"I Became a Christian and All I Got Was This Lousy T-Shirt is the funniest and most sincere spiritual growth book I've ever experienced. If you've never known the joy of walking with Christ, Vince's humor will entertain you as the truth of God's love will melt you. This book will grab you from the first page and won't let go until you're closer to Jesus.

"Vince's writing is hauntingly authentic, gut-wrenchingly funny, and profoundly spiritual. I had no idea I could laugh so hard, be moved so deeply, and crave Jesus more and more—all from reading one book."

Craig Groeschel, founding and senior pastor,
LifeChurch.tv; author, *Chazown*

"I don't want to hear the same truths regurgitated in the same ways over and over again. Tell me something I don't know. Challenge the way I think. Make me look in the mirror. And call me to a more Christ-centered life. I like Vince Antonucci for all of those reasons. His is a fresh voice in a world of tired ideas.

"This book will make you laugh and make you think. It will also make you reexamine your life. If you're serious about trading in your souvenir religion for authentic spiritual passion, this book is a must read."

Mark Batterson, lead pastor, National Community Church;
author, *In a Pit with a Lion on a Snowy Day*

"In *I Became a Christian and All I Got Was This Lousy T-Shirt*, my good friend Vince Antonucci tells my absolute favorite story of someone finding his way back to God—his own story. It's amazing! It's funny! It's a total God-thing! As Vince tells us his own story he also challenges us to live a life more authentically and fully following Christ. This is a book that will entertain you, inspire you, and help you experience everything God has for you. Read it and share it with a friend."

Dave Ferguson, lead pastor, Community Christian Church /
NewThing Network; author, *The Big Idea*

"Vince Antonucci is a powerful new voice for what it means to live an authentic Christian life today. He vividly describes a spiritual life filled with honesty, joy, humor, and conviction. Vince challenges us to stop trivializing our faith and pursue Jesus wholeheartedly. This book is a breath of fresh air!"

Jud Wilhite, senior pastor, Central Christian Church, Las Vegas;
author, *Stripped: Uncensored Grace on the Streets of Vegas*

"Some people have something worth saying, but they're as boring as the phone book. Other people are interesting, maybe even funny, but they are a few cards short in the deck of meaning. Vince is one of those rare pastors and writers who is both hilarious and substantial, and his faith isn't just a T-shirt: it's in his bones and marrow."

Brian D. McLaren, author (brianmclaren.net)

"Raucously humorous, Vince takes you on a journey toward authentically following Christ in a way that will have you laughing out loud one moment, then pondering biblical truth in a surprisingly fresh way the next. You won't put it down."

"Vince writes masterfully on his journey with Jesus and where it is taking him. He's a real deal kind of guy that I know and believe in. I loved it. I think we are seeing the emergence of a bright new author. This book is really good and is going to do a lot of good."

"Refreshing, hysterical, insightful . . . real!

"Vince does a great job reminding those of us who have been around the church a long time to take a new look at it, to see it from a non-Christians perspective, to look at our 'Christian life' and ask, 'Would anyone want what we have?'

"It would be a great book to hand to a new Christian. His practical look at what a 'true' relationship with Jesus really looks like would save many a new believer from years of 'stumbling around' trying to figure it all out."

"In *I Became a Christian and All I Got Was This Lousy T-Shirt*, Vince Antonucci gives an uplifting, insightful, and helpful recall of why following Jesus is worth all we have to give."

"A church without this book is like a kitchen without a church key (a.k.a. bottle opener): faith gets still and functional rather than sparkling and fun."

"I can't remember a time when I've been so encouraged and challenged by the same book. If you're serious about learning how to follow Jesus in the real world, you must read this."

"Vince Antonucci's personality comes through in his writing; as a person and as an author he is both refreshing and challenging. This book entertains and captivates, I found myself laughing out loud as I read, but more importantly this book will convict, even dare you to take a fresh look at how you see your faith."

"Vince Antonucci is one of the most riveting communicators I know. At every opportunity, he speaks passionately and convincingly about the church's role in reaching people far from God . . . because he was one. As you read this book, you won't stop laughing at Vince's twisted view of the world, at least until he nails you in the forehead with a life-disturbing truth. This book will transform Christian culture, and I'll be one of the first to take off my T-shirt."

For you, friend! Enjoy! Anita

I Became a Christian and All I Got Was This Lousy T-Shirt

Replacing Souvenir Religion
with Authentic Spiritual Passion

Vince Antonucci

BakerBooks
Grand Rapids, Michigan

© 2008 by Vince Antonucci

Published by Baker Books
a division of Baker Publishing Group
P.O. Box 6287, Grand Rapids, MI 49516-6287
www.bakerbooks.com

Printed in the United States of America

Library of Congress Cataloging-in-Publication Data
Antonucci, Vince.
    I became a Christian and all I got was this lousy t-shirt : replacing souvenir religion with authentic spiritual passion / Vince Antonucci.
        p.   cm.
    Includes bibliographical references.
    ISBN 978-0-8010-6818-8 (pbk.)
    1. Spirituality. I. Title.
BV4501.3.A58 2008
248.4—dc22   2007038975

In some cases, personal names have been changed to protect privacy.

In keeping with biblical principles of creation stewardship, Baker Publishing Group advocates the responsible use of our natural resources. As a member of the Green Press Initiative, our company uses recycled paper when possible. The text paper of this book is comprised of 30% post-consumer waste.

To Jen

Helen Keller once wrote,
"Life is either a daring adventure or nothing at all."
I want to live life, experience the adventure,
and follow Jesus with you.

CONTENTS

PART 1

DIGRESS

I CAME, I SAW, I BOUGHT THE T-SHIRT

My parents never took me to church.

Not once.

That might have something to do with the fact that my mother is Jewish and my father a professional gambler, but regardless, growing up I knew nothing of God, Jesus, or Christianity; as far as I know, I never even met a Christian.

I first heard about Jesus as a college sophomore in Buffalo, New York. It was Easter morning. I was waiting for my chronically late girlfriend to show up at my dorm room so we could go out for brunch. I turned on the TV. We had only three channels, and each one featured a dumb religious show. I would have turned it back off, but one of these shows looked potentially comical. An old man sat, or sunk really, into a big, red-leather chair. Questions flooded my mind: *How old is this guy? Is he going to live through this program? Had he become physically incapable of getting out of that chair? Shouldn't someone help him?*

Then Old Man spoke, "We've been studying the last week of Jesus Christ's life. Today we're going to talk about . . ." He named something, but I don't remember what. "Now most scholars believe," he continued, "that this event happened on *Tuesday* of Jesus' last week, but today I will prove to you through the evidence that it actually occurred on *Wednesday* of Jesus' last week."

I mulled this over for some time. Finally I decided: yes, this was the stupidest thing I had ever heard. I didn't know a thing about Jesus, but Tuesday or Wednesday? About something that happened thousands of years ago? If it happened at all? C'mon! I turned off the TV in disgust.

My girlfriend knocked on the door.

We left for brunch.

But I could not stop thinking about Old Man. Why did he care if it happened on Tuesday or Wednesday? What did he mean by "evidence"? Did anyone help him get out of that chair?

That night I was sitting in my girlfriend's dorm room when I noticed a Bible on the shelf. "You have a Bible?" I asked. "Can I borrow it?"

"Someone gave that to me years ago. I've never opened it. You can have it," she scoffed.

That night I began reading. I had never touched a Bible. I expected it to be organized like my *TV Guide*—by day and time—because of the Tuesday or Wednesday debate that was apparently tearing up Christianity. I also assumed it would read like a tall tale: "Once upon a time there was a man named Jesus, who could walk on water. He had a blue ox named Babe and could lasso a tornado!"

I was surprised by what I found. The Bible was full of historical accounts, and then I realized there would be evidence. I knew I could prove or disprove the Bible.

As I continued to read I discovered the Bible's outlandish claim that there was a God who loved me and sent Jesus for me. I learned that this God allegedly wanted a relationship with me and that he promised real and eternal life through Jesus.

And I encountered the followers of Jesus. I saw how the people who followed Jesus were fully alive, how they were consumed by the adventure of following Jesus. The passion and danger and excitement and joy of their new lives popped off of every page.

And I knew that I had to know: Is it true or a hoax? Did this actually happen? Is life like that really possible? Or did I just read a well-concocted fairy tale?

After months of reading and researching the Bible, I became convinced that it was true.

And I found myself drawn to Jesus. I didn't want to, but I couldn't help it. He was the coolest person I had ever come across. His character, his personality, his sense of humor, his sense of mission, his priorities, the way he was so subversive.

I still didn't know any Christians but decided I wanted to be one. Actually, that's an understatement. It wasn't just that I decided to become a Christian; it was like Jesus invaded my heart. I realized my entire life had been wrong, but God loved me anyway and was offering me a second chance. I had a grace explosion. I was *wrecked*.

Summer came and I decided to flee Buffalo and visit my father in Florida. He had just gotten out of prison (for embezzling money from Ted Williams, the famous baseball player, but that's another story). I told my dad that I had decided to become a Christian, though I had never met one. He was a little taken aback. After collecting his thoughts, he told me about a pastor who had visited him in jail, and wondered would I like to meet him. That night the pastor and I met and the next day I was baptized.

Before the water had evaporated from my skin, the pastor asked me, "So, where will you go to church when you get back home?"

I gave him my best Gary Coleman "What'chu talkin' 'bout, Willis?" look and said, "I haven't really thought about going to church. I don't think church is for me."

He claimed that church was for everyone and gave me the name and number of a minister friend in Buffalo. "He's a good guy. Give him a call."

Back in Buffalo I stared at my phone. The idea of going to church weirded me out. I was so nervous my fingers trembled as I dialed. I had to start and stop about four times. Finally there was a ring, and a kind female voice answered on the other end. I asked to speak to the pastor, and she informed me that he wasn't there.

"Oh," I said, disappointed.

"What's the matter?" she asked.

"Well, I'm supposed to come to church this Sunday."

"He will be here on Sunday," she answered. "Why don't you come and you can meet him then?"

"But how will I get in?"

"How will you get *in*?" She sounded confused.

"Yes, how will I get in?" I asked again.

"Do you mean how will you get *here*? I can give you directions."

"No," I responded, "how will I get in?"

"How will you get *in*?" she echoed.

I was starting to get angry. "Yes, how will I get in? I don't have an invitation. I haven't signed up, or—or anything."

Silence.

Finally she replied, "Well, you just walk in. Just show up and walk in."

This didn't make sense to me. Just show up and walk in? You couldn't just show up at a college and expect to participate in a class. A boy can't just show up at Cub Scouts without taking a three-finger pledge. Just show up and walk in?

I took a deep breath and resolved to speak slowly and gently. "So, what you're trying to tell me . . . is that I can drive to your church on Sunday . . . get out of my car . . . walk up to the door . . . and just . . . walk in."

"Yes, that is what I told you," she said. "Just show up and walk in."

"But . . . that's the strangest thing I've ever heard."

"And you," she responded, "are the strangest person I've ever talked to."

I was nervous. Going to church was a little like what happens in the movie *Antwone Fisher* where Antwone goes as an adult to meet his family for the first time. Except I'm not black, don't know Denzel Washington, and I'm not in the military. Okay, it was almost nothing like that movie. But I was nervous.

That Sunday I went to church for the first time.

And while I was nervous, I was also excited. I couldn't wait to meet Christians. Growing up, I had a vague negative stereotype of them formed mostly from watching Ned Flanders on *The Simpsons*. But now I knew the truth. After reading the New Testament, I knew what they would really be like. People with fire in their souls. People determined to change the world for Jesus. People filled with awe at what God is doing in their lives. People who can't stop being amazed by grace. People with joy oozing out of them. People who will follow Jesus wherever he goes. After months of reading the New Testament, I knew this is what Christians would be like. I couldn't wait to see in person, in the flesh, these lives that had become so familiar to me through the pages of the Bible.

I showed up that first Sunday . . .

took a deep breath . . .

and walked in . . .

EMILY

2

Walking through the front door of that church building was like passing through a portal to a different world. So much was unfamiliar. For the first time I heard about "propitiation," "puppet ministry," and "potluck suppers." I stood for "fellowship," knelt for prayer, and sat on a hard wooden bench (which they called a "pew"). I saw more polyester in one morning than I had my entire life. I experienced church snack time, which consisted of little pieces of cracker and small plastic shot glasses of grape juice. A man explained that we would be singing hymns 11, 52, 17, and 63. I almost yelled out, "Bingo!"

But it's now seventeen years later. I've gotten married (not to my chronically late girlfriend). I have two kids. I've gained a few pounds. And I've gone from having never walked into a church to having seventeen years worth of Sundays in church buildings. And with all that experience (not to mention the few extra pounds) under my belt, I can tell you that there is something very familiar about most of the Christians I've met. Unfortunately, it's not that they remind me of the people who populate the pages of Scripture. Instead, they remind me of a little girl named Emily.

Little Emily looks cute in her souvenir shirt that proclaims, "My parents went to Florida and all I got was this lousy T-shirt." But there's something sad about it too. She missed the journey. She didn't get to take part in the adventure. While others broke out of their dull routine, Emily missed the excitement of doing something different. She didn't get to play in the waves or hug Mickey. She didn't get to experience the joy. Even the horrifying incident when the tire blew out and Stan, the self-proclaimed "Good Samaritan Redneck," rescued the family in his *Sanford and Son* pickup truck has quickly become a fond memory for everybody. Everyone except Emily. She missed the journey.

As I've gone to church and met Christians and lived as one myself, I've realized something.

We are Emily.

When I read about the lives of the first Christians in the pages of the New Testament I see people who actually went "on vacation to Florida," who truly experienced the ups and downs of the trip. But when I look around at Christians today, I see people who just wear a T-shirt for an adventure they've missed out on. We're missing the journey. We're stuck in the same dull routine. We're missing out on the joy and fear and laughter and doubt and mystery and confusion of following Jesus, of taking great risks for God, of praying dangerous prayers, even of being spiritually attacked.

We wander around with lifeless shark eyes.

The more honest among us find ourselves asking questions like: Is this all there is? Is this really what Jesus meant when he said, "I have come that they may have life, and have it to the full"?[1] Is this the life Jesus died for me to have? Didn't Jesus pay too high a price to buy me *this* life? Am I just supposed to be miserable until I get to heaven?

I think the word that best describes how many feel about their Christian lives is not *abundant, joyful,* or *purpose-driven,* but *disappointing.*

And when I met Christians for the first time as a sophomore in college, I was disappointed. I was disappointed at *their* disappointment. And I swore I would never be like that.

But I have to be honest.

Over the years I have, at times, descended into the world of the "T-shirt wearers." I have found myself going through the motions. I've lost my purpose and passion for so long at times, I had to put them on the back of a milk carton. In honest moments I've asked those same despairing questions. I've been disappointed.

And I've wondered if maybe God is the problem. I mean, he does want everyone to say yes to his offer. And if someone is trying to sell me a new car, vacuum cleaner, or cell phone, I don't expect them to be completely honest. They'll exaggerate the benefits, ignore the problems. It may still be a great car, vacuum, or phone, but I'm not getting the whole truth, and I know it.

Maybe God is like that.

The benefits he claims to give to those who say yes to him include abundant life, pure joy in the face of trials, peace that surpasses understanding, power to heal the sick with our prayers, assurance that we will never be tempted in a way we can't handle, fearlessness, and the promise that we will do greater things than Jesus did.

How many Christians would say these things are a good description of their lives? More personally, does it describe yours?

So maybe God is the problem. Perhaps he's just a master salesman. After all, he's good at everything else.

But I don't think so.

Actually, I think *we're* the problem.

And I think there's a solution.
I think we need to go on vacation.

~~~

Last fall my family decided to go to Disney World.
From the moment we decided to go, things changed
around our house. A sense of anticipation started brew-
ing. We breathed hope. I'd return from a bad day at work
and tell my wife, "My life sucks." She'd smile and say,
"Yes, honey, but we're going on vacation!" As our trip
neared, the excitement boiled. I picked up a book on
Disney to prepare. This book had scientific equations
and mathematical algorithms to help avoid lines and go
on the most rides in one day. I spent hours planning in
detail each of our days at Disney. I determined the order
of the rides we would go on, where we would eat, when
my kids would go to the bathroom. Nothing was left to
chance. It was a lot of work, but it was fun because it
helped me look forward to our vacation.

Finally the day arrived. We loaded up the car and
raced away from home. Pulling out of the driveway felt
like a prison break from my worries and stress. At home
and work so much competes for my attention and so
many problems weigh me down. But as we drove away
my blood pressure went from boil to simmer, my heart
rate from Metallica to Michael Bolton. The five-hundred-
pound gorilla I'd been giving a piggyback ride kindly
climbed off my shoulders. And I realized that, at least
for the next week, I'd be able to relax.

Not only that, I would have fun. Part of the reason I
love vacations is because they can be a journey out of
routine and into adventure. I like having some standardi-
zation in my schedule, but oftentimes my entire life
feels like a monotonous, never-ending routine. But as
our neighborhood disappeared in the rearview mirror,

I knew I was also leaving my routine behind, and we were driving into an adventure. Even though I had done my normal manic, control-freak planning, there was still some uncertainty about our trip. I wasn't sure exactly how things would go down, what we might experience, or who we'd encounter. It was going to be a blast.

I *love* vacation.

Now don't get me wrong, I'm not saying that vacations are nonstop thrills or that they're perfect. Parts of every vacation are *boring*. The drive to Disney took twelve hours—twelve hours, with two small children. In case you're keeping score, that's three meals, four snacks, eight bathroom stops, and forty-seven *thousand* "Are we there yets?" The trip was pretty boring. But that was okay. This was boredom with a purpose. Because we were going somewhere, we had a destination, and we knew it would be exciting.

Vacations can also be just plain *bad* at times. One day on that perfectly designed Disney trip, we arrived at the park early, according to plan. We were first in line and waiting for the grand opening. Finally they opened the gates and everyone went running in, with us in the lead. The entire crowd was rushing for the same ride, knowing that later it would have the longest lines. They longed for what only I would achieve. We would be first on that ride, and then first on the next most popular ride, and then first on the next most popular ride. Our plan was working perfectly. There was no stopping us now! After about a hundred yards I looked back to gloat, but I noticed that the thousands of people following me were no longer following me. They had all turned right, but we were still going straight. I saw a Disney employee and asked, "What's going on? Isn't *this* how you get to the big ride?" "No," he said, pointing to the throng of people, "*that's* how you get to the big ride." My whole plan . . . ruined.

We went on another vacation years earlier that was full of problems. I was speaking at a conference in Chicago in late April, and we decided to fly out a couple of days early to make it into a vacation. We were stoked . . . until the day we left.

I woke up with the flu *and* pink eye. Freakin' pink eye! How do you even get pink eye? I was miserable the entire flight. We brought my son, who was just a baby then, and he was miserable on the plane. This meant *everyone* was miserable on the plane. When we arrived and picked up our rental car, it was the longest automobile I'd ever seen. We drove off in the Pimpmobile, embarrassed but accepting our fate. Pimpin' ain't easy, but someone's got to do it.

The next day we drove to downtown Chicago and took our son to the aquarium where we discovered babies are not interested in fish. We left the aquarium and went to a supposedly great restaurant, but we didn't like our food. After dinner we went to a Bulls game where my son decided he didn't want to sit on my lap. He kept escaping and crawling under the legs of total strangers, so we left in the second quarter.

The next morning my son was sick. He had the flu . . . and pink eye. Freakin' pink eye! We decided that sickness would not stop us, so we drove to legendary Wrigley Field for a Cubs game. It was 34 degrees and the wind chill made it feel like we were stuck in the middle of a Popsicle. We left in the second inning. On the drive back to our hotel it felt like something was stuck in my tooth, so I scratched at it, and my tooth chipped. Well, it didn't *chip* as much as it *chunked*. There was more tooth in my hand than in my mouth. And now every time I spoke, the jagged spear that once was my tooth cut the inside of my mouth. That night we went to an Italian restaurant a friend told us about. As I pulled into a parking place, I misjudged the length of the Pimpmobile and clipped the corner of the car next to me. It was a brand-new Mercedes Benz. We left a note on the car, hoping the owner would decide it wasn't worth the trouble to follow up. We dragged ourselves over to the restaurant but realized it was way too fancy for us. This was made clear by the sign on the door which read:

No shirt.
No shoes.
No *you*.
(Yes you, Sabertooth. So take your pink eye, bloody mouth, sick kid, miserable wife and go to McDonald's.)

We went to McDonald's.

After dinner our son was so sick we decided to take him to the emergency room. When we finally arrived back at our hotel, the people who owned the Mercedes were waiting for us to exchange insurance information.

The next morning my wife woke up with the flu. And pink eye. Freakin' pink eye!

You get my point. Vacations aren't always fun and games.

But I've noticed that there's something different about the problems I experience on vacation. For some reason, they become fun stories to share. It's strange. The problems I experience in my every day life are just problems. But when I look back at the problems we've experienced on vacations, they're things we talk and laugh about now.

I'm not sure why. Perhaps it's because we had a purpose. The boring or bad part interrupted our mission, but we still had a purpose.

Or it could be that I wasn't alone. I was doing the vacation with people I love. And that sense of community helped me deal with the boredom and problems and to laugh about it later.

Or maybe problems on a vacation are different because there's a finish line to the vacation. And that finish line allowed me to view the problem in the context of the entire vacation rather than getting obsessed with it, like it's everything.

I'm not sure why, but the bad and boring parts of my vacations are okay because they're all part of the adventure. Typically we tell stories and laugh about them later.

I love vacation.

And, when I'm really living it, I love the Christian life. It's helped me to approach my days with a sense of anticipation, and it's allowed me to break out of my routines and experience adventure.

But, like a vacation, following Jesus is not a perfect life of nonstop thrills. There are some boring and bad parts. But still there's something different about them, simply because I'm following Jesus.

So why are so many Christians disappointed? Is it possible that we, like Emily, are missing out on the journey? Is Jesus calling us to live life with authentic spiritual passion, but we're just wearing the T-shirt, practicing a souvenir religion?

ALIVE

3

When I read the Bible I notice that Jesus didn't go around asking people to *believe* in him. It's what I would expect; it's just not what he did.

He also didn't ask people to *behave*. Again, it's what I would expect, but it's not really what he did.

Instead, he asked people to *follow him*. Here's the kind of thing Jesus did. One time he walked up to some dude who was in the middle of work and said, "Hey, follow me." And this guy did it!

If Jesus were here today, I doubt it'd be different. I don't think he'd ask me to believe in him. He'd ask me to *follow* him. According to Jesus, being a Christian is not so much about believing or behaving correctly as it is about traveling with him. Jesus is going somewhere and he wants me to go with him.

Jesus even made a promise to those who follow: "I have come that you may have life, and have it to the full."[1] I love the way one of the early Christians expressed this. About 150 years after Jesus, this guy named Irenaeus wrote, "The glory of God is man fully alive . . ."[2] The idea is that God loves it when we are fully alive. Jesus came so we can be fully alive. And he's saying in John 10:10, "If you follow me, I can make you fully alive."

So this has got me wondering: Where exactly is Jesus going? Where is he inviting me to go? And is it possible that a lot of us are believing and behaving, but we're missing out on what Christianity is really about—which is following Jesus. And maybe that's why we're not quite fully alive.

Maybe that's why more of us are wearing the T-shirt instead of experiencing a passionate journey with him.

And, as I said, I've been thinking that maybe what Jesus is calling us to is kind of like a lifelong vacation with him.

⟋⟍

Looking back at my life before I started following Jesus, I totally lacked a sense of expectation. I didn't have hope or excitement for the future. Things were okay, but I didn't see why they would get better. That one-eightied when I started following Jesus. I discovered that God had plans for my life, and I often had no idea what he was planning. And so I began to live each day with a sense of anticipation, wondering what God might be up to, how he might make this day amazing.

The Bible is full of talk about walking with God, walking with Jesus, walking with God's Spirit. That tells me that I better buy some good sneakers, because I'm going somewhere. I think where we're going is out of our ruts and into an adventure.

My life became a crazy adventure that I could never have even imagined when I started following Jesus. Sometimes it's been dramatic events like leaving law school to start a radical church or flying with a group to Vietnam to meet with government officials, asking them to give their people religious freedom. But more often it's just been everyday kind of stuff, like surprising the dishwasher at a restaurant with a twenty-dollar tip, or offering to pray with a co-worker, or looking for an opportunity to share God's love with the girl who cuts my hair, or finding a teachable moment with my kids where I get to help them understand the most important story ever told. Following Jesus is an adventure.

Following Jesus also relieves stress. I find that when I get in the car or airplane for a vacation I leave my worries and stress behind. And that's a glorious, choir-of-angels, smiling-haloed-babies-floating-around-me-in-golden-diapers feeling. But when I get back in the car or airplane and return home, my worries and stress are still there. They've been waiting. They've by now claimed squatter's rights on my house. And the reunion with my worries and stress is always a gruesome, funeral-dirge, greenish-baby-poop-falling-out-of-the-diapers-right-on-my-head feeling. And so a vacation is a nice, temporary reprieve from my worry and stress, though it's no long-term solution.

But when I'm following Jesus, there's a permanent, permeating sense of peace that happens deep inside. Jesus promised, "Come to me, all you who are weary and burdened, and I will give you rest. Take my yoke upon you and learn from me, for I am gentle and humble in heart, and you will find rest for your souls. For my yoke is easy and my burden is light."[3] The idea is that Jesus doesn't necessarily remove my suitcases of worries and stress; instead he helps me carry them.

God tells those who follow Jesus that he will give them a peace that defies understanding. If I follow Jesus I should have peace even in the worst of times, even in the middle of stress, even when there are a million things to worry about. And that's easy to dismiss as just trite Christian talk, except that it's true. I have watched people deal with all kinds of problems—a wife losing her husband of less than a year to cancer, a husband discovering his wife was sleeping with their neighbor each Sunday while he was at church, parents dealing with the death of their sixteen-year-old daughter in a car accident, a family losing their house and all their belongings to a fire, a father having to watch his son be attacked and eaten by a shark—and the ones who were really following Jesus did it with a peace I could not understand.

See, my saying Jesus is calling us to a vacation does not mean it's a perfect life of nonstop thrills. There are still some boring and bad parts. But there's something different about them. I'm not sure why. Perhaps it's because we have a purpose now . . . we're part of something bigger, so our problems don't seem so magnified. Or maybe it's because we have the support of a community of faith and of a God who can transform our attitude and carry our burdens. It could be that we now have a finish line, and we know that our suffering will end as well, and there's a sense of anticipation about what comes next.

⌒

Jesus asks people to follow him. He's going somewhere, and he wants us to go with him. He promises that those who follow will experience life fully alive.

A lot of us have been believing and behaving, just not following. Like little Emily, we're a part of the family, but we're missing out on the vacation, the journey, the adventure.

So what is this life we're being called to?

Here's the best I can figure. The life God authored for us and offers to us, is this:

To live life with Jesus, and to live the Jesus life.

To live life with Jesus is about the inward life. It's me experiencing the presence of Jesus. It's soaking in all of him that's out there. It's God impressing himself on me. It's God changing me.

To live the Jesus life is about the outward life. It's me being the presence of Jesus. It's releasing out all of him that's in here. It's God expressing himself through me. It's God changing the world with me.

Since moving to Virginia Beach, I've developed allergies. Recently my wife bought a humidifier for our bedroom. Each morning I have to fill the thing up with water, and the rest of the day it releases that water into the air. I've learned that the humidifier can be turned on and running hard, but it accomplishes absolutely nothing if it's not filled with water.

The Christian life is something like that humidifier. I admit it's a simple analogy, but it helps convey the give-and-take there is in following Jesus. Repeatedly I need to be filled up with Jesus (which happens as I live life with Jesus), and then I need to continuously release Jesus (which happens as I live the Jesus life). I release Jesus because my purpose is to serve others, to touch them with God's love. But I can only do that if I'm filled with Jesus. Otherwise I can run hard, but I won't accomplish anything.

We've been invited to live life with Jesus and to live the Jesus life. To do that, we need to understand what it means and overcome what holds us back. Then we can lose the T-shirt and experience the adventure.

PART 2

UNDRESS

TAKING OFF THE SHIRT

ABIDE

4

I'm considering making and marketing a bumper sticker to Christians that says: "Stop Having a Relationship with Jesus." I doubt it would sell, and to be honest I wouldn't buy it either, but one of our biggest problems, it seems to me, is this whole idea of a relationship with Jesus.

———

I have a relationship with a guy named Kevin. We met in a small group I was leading and instantly hit it off. We started playing pool, watching sports together, and serving side-by-side. Eventually we became best friends. I have a great relationship with Kevin. But Kevin moved away three years ago. Since then I only talk to him once or twice a month.

I wish he lived closer. It'd be nice if I could see him more. I miss him.

But I'm fine without him. Not having him around hasn't dramatically impacted me for the worse. It certainly hasn't ruined my life.

Why not?

Because we have a relationship. It's a great relationship, but it's *just* a relationship.

I have a relationship with Jesus. We met, oddly enough, in Buffalo, New York. It took me awhile to get to know him, but I grew to like him. We began sharing life together in deep ways. I've celebrated with him, and grasped for his hand when things were falling apart.

I have a great relationship with Jesus.

But sometimes I do life in such a way that I go without Jesus. I don't take time to pray or to read the Bible. I can go entire days not talking to or thinking about him much, if at all. And when I go without Jesus, I wish he were closer. It'd be nice if I could see him more. I miss him. But I *can* live life without him. Things certainly don't go as well, but not keeping him around doesn't ruin my life.

Why not?

Because we have a relationship. It's a great relationship, but it's *just* a relationship.

When I read the Bible, I don't think Jesus was exactly talking about us having a relationship with him. I do think a relationship with Jesus is better than a *religion* with Jesus. A lot of people are not living life fully alive because they have a *religion* with Jesus. To them, it's all about believing and behaving. Their theology is lined up right and their actions are mostly right, and so they feel like they're basically pleasing God, and they're better than most of the people around, and someday they'll probably get into heaven. But deep inside they're empty. The one thing their life is missing is *life*, because Jesus came to give life, but it doesn't come through religion. His ultimate goal isn't to get people to believe and behave. And so, while others experience an adventure with Jesus, they just attend church.

A relationship with Jesus is better than a religion with Jesus, but still, I don't think Jesus was talking about us just having a relationship with him.

For instance, one time Jesus said, "*Abide* in Me, and I in you. As the branch cannot bear fruit of itself, unless it *abides* in the vine, so neither can you, unless you *abide* in Me. I am the vine, you are the branches; he who *abides* in Me, and I in him, he bears much fruit; for apart from Me you can do nothing."[1] To abide in means to *live within*. Jesus says he wants me to live inside of him, and that he will live inside of me. That doesn't sound like a relationship to me.

What if you could somehow interview a baby inside his mother's womb? And let's say you asked the baby, "Do you have a *relationship* with your mother?"

I think the baby would give you a really weird look. Now from the pictures I've seen, babies in their mothers' wombs look very alienlike, so you may not realize the baby was giving you a weird look. But trust me; this question would get you a weird look.

The baby would say, "Could you repeat that?" (I'm assuming this baby can speak.)

So you ask again, "I said, do you have a *relationship* with your mother?"

The baby would give you another weird look and answer, "That's what I thought you said, but I can't believe you would ask that. How do I answer? I mean yes, we do have a relationship, but c'mon it's *way* beyond that. I mean, I live *inside of her*. I can't live *without her*. I am totally *dependent on her* for everything that keeps me alive. I can't do *anything without her*. So yes, I guess we have a relationship, but that's a colossal understatement." (I'm assuming this baby uses cool words like *colossal*.)

"I think the next time you make your way into a womb for an interview," the baby would conclude, "you should think of more sensible questions. I'm sorry, I have to go now—the *Maury Povich* show is about to come back on and the paternity tests are in." (I'm assuming there are little TVs in mom's bellies and that babies like to watch Maury Povich because he often reveals the identity of the real father.)

So when we pray to God about our *relationship* with him, I imagine God saying, "Did you really just say that? I mean, yes, I guess it is a relationship, but you did catch the part where I said I want us to live inside each other, right? You want to call that a *relationship*? You can call it what you want, but I'm inviting you into *much* more than a relationship. I'm offering to be the womb you exist within, and the blood that flows through your veins. I want to be the umbilical cord that brings you the fluids that sustain you, and I want to be those fluids that sustain you. I want to be the breath that enters your lungs when you're born, and I want to be your lungs. What I want is for you to get lost inside of me, and I want to be lost inside of you. My desire is for us to be *one*. Now, if you'll excuse me, I have to go—*Sanford and Son* is on." (I'm assuming there's a big TV in heaven, and that God likes to watch *Sanford and Son*.)

What God was describing before he started watching TV, that's what I want. But too often what I have is more of just a relationship with Jesus. And when I don't abide and *really* live life with Jesus, my life gets pretty messed up. I have something less than a full life.

⌒

One of the most messed-up times in my life came as a result of complications during my wife's second pregnancy. There was nonstop upchucking and multiple stays in the hospital, and my life started spiraling around the commode like a dead goldfish at its funeral, and then was flushed right down the toilet. Finally, I admitted to my friend Kevin how bad I was doing. He came over that night to hang out. I explained how for the past month or two I had drifted away from God and had barely taken any time to read the Bible or pray. I didn't have much time available, with all the vomit and baby poop flying around the house, but I didn't even take the opportunities I did have to spend with God.

"Well," Kevin said, "when I leave tonight, read the Bible and pray."

"I'll be honest," I sighed, "right now I wouldn't even know what to read in the Bible. I wouldn't know where to begin."

"Okay," he said, "read the book of James."

"Fine," I answered, wanting him to leave.

So he left. Not wanting to have lied to my friend's face, I picked up a Bible and turned to James. I started to read, but I wasn't feeling it.

James 1:1 says, "James, a servant of God and of the Lord Jesus Christ, To the twelve tribes scattered among the nations: Greetings."

I said, in the general direction of God, *Oh, that's real helpful. I'm a changed man! Woo hoo!*

James 1:2 says, "Consider it pure joy, my brothers, whenever you face trials of many kinds."

Now I was getting mad. I shot back, *My wife is in the hospital. I've got so much going on I can't handle it all. Why would I consider this pure joy? You've got to be kidding me.*

James 1:3 says, "Because you know that the testing of your faith develops perseverance."

This is unbelievable, I thought. *As far as I can see, this testing of my faith isn't developing anything.*

James 1:4 says, "Perseverance must finish its work so that you may be mature and complete, not lacking anything."

I almost yelled, *Here we go! I mean, this is my problem, right here. If I knew that all the things I'm going through were*

*helping me to become "mature and complete," maybe then I
could deal with it, but I don't. And it says "not lacking anything." God, you tell me, what am I lacking that you're trying
to complete in me by what I'm going through? Huh?*

God answered me. It was really weird. I didn't hear a
voice or anything like that, but it might have been less
weird if I had. Suddenly, as soon as "Huh?" came out,
I understood. I knew what was wrong. I realized why I
had to go through all the junk that had been occurring
in my life, and how it *could* bring me to a better place.

The problem, I realized, was that I wasn't living life
with Jesus. I wasn't *abiding*.

When I first started following Jesus I really lived life with
him. I *was* abiding in him. But over time it became just
a relationship. There were many other things supporting
me, giving me joy and peace and contentment. Take my
schedule, for example: going to sleep, getting up, going to
work, eating at the same time each day. That gave me a
sense of comfort. Another was getting a lot of work done.
Checking things off my to-do list made me feel good about
myself. Money—having a little extra in savings provided a
sense of security. TV—getting to watch my favorite shows
supplied my joy. And there were other things too.

When my wife got sick, all the other things that were
supporting me got taken away. My routine was gone. I
was no longer getting much work done. The money in
my savings account was sent to the hospital to pay the
mounting bills. I had no time to watch TV.

I should have been able to lose all that and still be
fine. But I was *not* fine.

The problem was this: I wasn't abiding in Jesus. All we
had was a relationship. And, as with any relationship,
life got in the way.

I need to live life with Jesus. I need to abide.

The truth is I have trouble abiding.

Why? Read on . . .

36

AKA

5

Twenty weeks into our first pregnancy we learned that we were having a boy. We got out a blank piece of paper and started writing down potential names. This is difficult business. We applied a variety of tests. *#1*: The "Has my wife ever dated someone with this name?" test. *#2*: The "How will other kids make fun of him?" test. Trajan was one of my favorites until my wife pointed out the obvious condom association. *#3*: The "What does the name actually mean?" test. We had settled on "Cade" until my wife learned it means "Lumpy." "There is no way I'm having a son named Lumpy!" she yelled. I considered this ironic since her name is Porky, but I didn't mention that. (Okay, her name isn't Porky, but that would be totally ironic.) *#4*: The "Banana Fana" test. We sang each name out in song,

> Cade, Cade, Bo Bade
> Banana, Fana, Fo Fade
> Fee Fy Mo Made
> Cade!

The purpose of the test is to see if the name leads to cursing. This test eliminated Mitch, Buck, and, of course, Fastard. #5: The "Pig Latin" test. We had to make sure the name sounded cool in Pig Latin because some day Pig Latin will be our national language. (When it does, tell 'em Incevay Ntonucciaay told you first.) Finally, we agreed on a name . . . Dawson Cade Antonucci. (Apparently it's fine with my wife if he's lumpy in the middle. . . . Just like his daddy.)

Growing up, I had a vague sense that something was not right about *my* name. Something seemed off about my identity. I couldn't explain it. I wasn't sure why I felt that way.

Finally, the answer came out. Actually, the answer came *down* . . . from my mother's attic.

I was fifteen, applying for my first job and would need a social security number. My mother told me that I didn't have a social security number. I was confused; all my friends had social security numbers. She brought a box of old documents down from the attic, sat me down, and told me about the circumstances of my birth.

When I was born my father believed the FBI was after him. My father, whose paranoia made Howard Hughes look sane, decided that if he registered at the hospital under his real name (Vincent Antonucci), SWAT teams would come busting in from every direction. And so he registered under, and then gave me the name, Vincent Shuffle. Remember, he was a professional poker player. Later he went out and had a fake birth certificate made for me with the name Vincent Antonucci. My parents used this fake birth certificate to enroll me in school, Little League, and so on. But now I needed a social security number, and we had a problem.

My mother suggested that I file for a name change and make my legal name Vincent Antonucci, which I had been using all along anyway. And so we did the paperwork, went and saw a judge, and at the age of fifteen I had a new, but old, name.

At the age of twenty I *again* discovered that all along I had been going by the wrong name. As I studied the old documents found in the Bible, I realized that it didn't matter what my parents had or hadn't named me; God had a name for me.

Throughout the Bible we see God changing people's names. Abram becomes Abraham. Jacob becomes Israel. Simon becomes Peter. Saul becomes Paul. My favorite name change happens with John. John was a fisherman Jesus chose to be one of the twelve disciples in his inner circle. He wrote the Gospel of John. In his account of Jesus' life, a phrase comes up repeatedly that is not found in any of the other Gospels. John refers to "the one Jesus loved" or "the disciple whom Jesus loved." Here's the kicker. John was referring to *himself*. "The one Jesus loved" had become his identity.

I think that should be my identity. I think that should be your identity too. More than anything else, we are the ones Jesus loves.

And now, finally, I knew I was not Vincent Shuffle or Vincent Antonucci. *I* was the one Jesus loves. That was my true identity.

The problem is that I struggled to feel loved by Jesus. And not feeling loved by Jesus created distance between us. It led to an inability to develop intimacy, to an unwillingness to abide. I was just in a cordial relationship with him. I was his employee and his buddy, but I didn't feel like the one Jesus loved.

Part of my problem was that my father had given me other names besides Shuffle. He was an angry, bitter person, and much of it came out at me. He was emotionally abusive. I repeatedly was told that I was stupid, bad, worthless. The soundtrack of my early years was filled with verses like "How could you be so dumb?" "What's wrong with you?" "Are you totally worthless?" "You've got a real problem." "Didn't I already tell you that? You really are stupid."

Those names shaped me. They left me feeling like my identity was "Stupid" . . . "Bad" . . . "Worthless."

And it wasn't just my dad. I did a lot through the years to live up to those names, and to even add a few of my own. I branded myself with names like "Disappointment" . . . "Manipulative" . . . "Selfish" . . . "Sinful."

Those names shaped me as well.

So how could I now accept my new name "the one Jesus loves"? The question consumed me: how could Jesus love me when I knew I was not worth loving?

Ironically, I couldn't accept the fact that Jesus loved *me*, but I kept sharing with my friends how Jesus loved *them*. In fact, all I wanted to do was talk to people about Jesus' love for them. Eventually that passion led me to become a pastor and then to start a new church called Forefront in Virginia Beach, Virginia. I had preached about ten times in my life prior to the first Sunday of the new church but was now in a position where I would be preaching week-in and week-out. I had to choose the themes for the three- to eight-week series we'd be doing, pick the weekly topics within those themes, and write the messages for those topics. And so I started choosing and picking and writing and preaching . . . and an odd thing happened. The message "You are loved by God.

God wants you, even if you don't feel wanted" started coming out of me over and over and over again.

It started on our very first Sunday when I talked about Madonna and how she lost her mother at a young age, which seems to have fueled her lifelong search for affirmation. I explained that God sent his Son so we might be adopted as his children, which seems especially appropriate for Madonna. I assured everyone, "Yes, God loves Madonna. And you know what? God loves you too."

I did a message where I explained that in the movie *X-Men* there are a group of people who are mutants. Something is seriously wrong with each of them. This causes the world to reject them. But Professor X wants them and views their mutant characteristics not as objects of scorn but as what makes them special and able to be used in great ways. God is just like that. We see this throughout the Bible.

God chose Abraham to be the father of faith, even though Abraham had a serious problem with lying. God chose to save Noah from the flood. We think, *Well, Noah must have been a perfect guy.* But after the flood we find Noah drunk, naked, and passed out like a frat boy after an all-night party. God chose Moses to represent him and be his spokesperson. Moses was a fugitive from the law because he had murdered a guy. God chose Rahab, a prostitute. He chose Gideon, a total scared wimp, to lead his army. He chose David, an adulterer. The list goes on and on.

God chooses mutants. He picks people with problems. And God is able to use them, often not *despite* their problems but *because* of them. And the truth, if we're honest, is that we're all mutants. "And so," I told our people, "do you know what that means? It means God loves you. God would pick you. God wants you."

Some time ago, I flew out to California to speak at a camp for troubled teens. My opening illustration on the

3

first night was about what life is like on the playground at school when you have to pick teams. The best-looking, most athletic two people designate themselves captains. They slowly size up the twenty or so kids and then start choosing their teams. First they pick the young gods of kickball. "I choose Billy, for Billy has been known to kick the ball so hard it deflates on contact. Billy, you shall play for me."

After the kickball warriors are gone, the two captains begin selecting their friends and the popular kids who are not so athletic. Next they barter over the non-descript kids—the nameless, faceless kids who make up the middle class of the school. After this group the only people remaining are . . . the final four. One is standing in his long johns. One has glasses so thick you can't see his eyes. One is famous for eating anything for a dollar. (Rumor has it he ate a piece of Dave's poop in third grade.) The last is picking his nose. All four are avoiding eye contact with anyone. They are used to being the last four, but they still don't like it. It takes the captains as long to choose from these final four as the previous sixteen combined. The first captain says, "Wow. Gosh. Umm. Huh. Yeah, I'll um, I'll um . . . I'll take Langdon."

"I'm Kreely."

"Yeah, whatever. Get over here."

Then the other captain, "Okay, yeah . . . umm, this is bad. I can't believe this, stink! Well, I'll take Kenny, as long as you don't cry, and promise never to touch the ball!"

That's the way it goes on the playground. But, I explain to the teens, "Listen to this: that is *not* how God chooses. God *starts* with the final four! God doesn't look at us the way the world does. God doesn't select people the way the world does. And do you know what that means? It means God wants you! God loves you!"

One time a radio station in Virginia Beach changed formats from rock to country. For some reason, as an interlude between the two formats, they played the same song over and over for two straight days. You'd talk to a friend on the phone or see someone at the store and they'd say, "Have you heard 93.7? They keep playing the same song over and over! You've got to check it out. It's like a train wreck on the air!" Everyone wondered how long it would continue.

Going to Forefront in our early years was very similar. People must have been asking, "When is this guy going to stop preaching on the same subject?" I hoped maybe a side benefit from the weekly emotional train wreck I was having in the pulpit was that it would create a good buzz in the community about our church. "Have you been to Forefront? The guy keeps preaching on the same topic over and over! You've got to check it out!"

After attending awhile, someone would come up to me in the lobby on a Sunday morning and say with a laugh, "Okay, Vince, you can stop preaching about that now. We get it."

I felt like throwing the person against a wall and screaming, "Well sorry, I don't!"

Even though I had become a Christian, even though I was preaching sermon after sermon on the topic, still I couldn't feel like I was the one Jesus loves, and it held me back from living life with him.

I continued to wrestle with the question: how could Jesus love me when I knew I wasn't worth loving?

Finally, the answer came out. Actually, the answer came *down*, again, from my mom's attic.

We were visiting my mother, who would soon be moving from our old house into a condo. She informed us that we'd be leaving with a bunch of stuff she had been saving for me. Soon it all came down—Legos, Matchbox cars, books, and . . . a teddy bear. It was *my* teddy bear, from when I was little. It was a mess. Years earlier, my mother had sewn an ear back on. She had done reconstructive surgery on its neck and back. It was missing fur around its eyes, on both feet, and on his back by the little music handle. It had a big scar across its head. The cutest thing was the four little pieces of fur missing from where my four fingers used to hold it constantly. My finger marks had become permanently embedded in my bear.

When I was little, I *loved* this bear. I carried it everywhere. My mother would turn the music handle and it would make music, bad music, but I would move in tight and that music would comfort me and lull me to sleep.

I *loved* this bear, but there was nothing *lovable*, nothing *valuable* about the bear in itself. Even when it was new it was obviously not an expensive stuffed animal. It probably cost a few dollars at the time. If you tried to sell it at a garage sale today you might ask for a quarter. It's just not valuable, except that it is to *me*, and especially back when I was a kid.

I loved this bear. But I didn't love it because it was valuable. I loved it because . . . I loved it. I loved it because it was *my* bear. My love was not based on its value, rather my love *made* this bear valuable. My love gave this bear significance. When I was a kid, you could have offered me a vacation to Disney World and I wouldn't have traded my bear for it. If my parents had held a yard sale back then and asked me how much we should sell my bear for, I would have said a million dollars . . . and that wouldn't have been enough. They would have said,

"Well, silly, it only cost us about two dollars, and it's gotten really beat up since then." I would have said, "I don't care. I won't sell it. It's *my* bear, and I love him." And finally I understood how Jesus could love me when I wasn't worth loving.

I realized that the love I had for my bear is essentially the same kind of love God has for me. It's not a love that loves because the object of the love is valuable; it's a love that *gives* value.

God knew me. He knew what I was worth in the beginning, he knew the damage that had been done to me over the years, he knew my current condition. But the most significant thing God knew about me was that I was his. I may have been beat up, pulled out of shape, ripped, and left with stuffing hanging out, but I was his. I may not have looked like much to anyone else, but I was his. And so he loved me. And his love gave me value, significance, and importance.

Now I have to admit, I still struggle with this sometimes. Because it's not just realizing that I'm loved. It's *living* it. It's abiding in Jesus, in his love, moment by moment. And I have good days and bad when it comes to living in his love. It's like I constantly need reminders.

⌒⌒

A few months after deciding on a name, my son was born. Two years later we had a baby girl. And each of my kids taught me the teddy bear lesson again. I had very little experience with babies but quickly learned that all they do is sleep, eat, and poop. These kids did nothing to deserve my love, but I loved them more than anything. Why? Because they were mine. I had no interest in anyone else's babies, but I loved mine, just because they were mine. They didn't have to do anything to deserve it. In fact, there was nothing they could do to make me love them any more than I did simply because they were mine, and I'm convinced there's nothing they could do that would make me love them any less.

The births of my kids were reminders of the teddy bear lesson. They taught me again that I could accept my true identity. And I decided that I wanted my children to have a built-in reminder so they wouldn't have to struggle like I do. I resolved that I would make my kids' primary identity "I am the one Jesus loves." I committed to saying it to them every day,

> "Do you know who you are? . . . You're the one Jesus loves."

In fact, I decided it would be the first words they would hear from my mouth. Immediately after birth, when the doctor handed my baby to me, I would say those words.

Finally that day arrived. April 22, 1999. We rushed to the hospital. We couldn't wait to have a baby, and I was excited to tell him who he was. But the delivery was not the joyous occasion I had envisioned. It became frightening and stressful. My son came out with the umbilical cord wrapped around his neck.

He was blue.

I walked away in fear, backwards, until my back hit a wall. I continued to watch from the corner of the room in horror. I begged God to make him okay. The doctors worked feverishly to revive him. And finally he was all right. Eventually they handed him to me. I took a deep breath, exhaled, and said, "Do you know who you are? You're the one Jesus loves."

Two years later, we drove to the same hospital for the same reason. This time we were having a girl. My wife and I were hanging out in the delivery room. Everything was great when suddenly the external monitor that displayed the baby's heart rate (which is supposed to stay between 120 and 160) dropped to 25. Inside the womb, our baby's heart had nearly stopped beating. Nurses and doctors came running in. People were yelling. A doctor broke my wife Jen's water, stuck an electrode in her, and attached it to our baby's head. He said this internal monitor would provide a more precise reading of the baby's heart rate. Finally, the heart rate went back up to normal and everyone left. But soon the heart rate dropped again. Doctors and nurses rushed in yelling. Then the pulse returned to normal. But less than an hour later it happened again. The doctor came in and said, "This baby needs to come out right now!"

I questioned him, "But you just told us she's not ready yet."

"She's ready enough," he said. "She has to be."

He turned to my wife and explained, "Jennifer, you can only push one time. You only get one push to get this baby out. Do you understand me?"

"Vince?" Jen said.

"It's gonna be okay," I assured her.

With our first child, Jen had pushed for thirty straight minutes. They had told her she was lucky, that sixty minutes was closer to average. The doctor said this time she would get just one push.

Jen asked, "Vince, what's going on?"

"I don't know," I answered. "Let's just pray."

So we prayed.

The doctor got in position. He said, "Okay Jen, you have one push, make it a good one."

Jen pushed.

The doctor said, "Good, just a little more," and the baby popped out.

With one push.

Then they discovered the problem. An umbilical cord is supposed to be connected to the middle of the placenta, and it twists in. But our daughter's umbilical cord was connected to the side of the placenta, and it wasn't twisted in. It was held to the placenta by a thin, loose piece of skin. The doctor explained that this is the cause of death for most stillborn babies with this condition. At that time, it was impossible to detect the situation with the umbilical cord, so when the mother starts pushing, it rips away from the placenta, and the baby can't survive.

The doctor said, "Jennifer, if you had pushed twice, I don't think your baby would have made it."

The nurse walked over to the bedside and whispered, "Listen, I don't know you two people, I don't know anything about you, or . . . what your faith is . . . but that had to be God who kept this baby alive. I've never seen anything like that. That was a miracle. There's no other reason this baby is alive right now."

I looked her in the eye and said, "We're Buddhists."

Finally they examined our daughter enough to know she was okay, and then handed her to me. I held her close and whispered, "Do you know who you are? You're the one Jesus loves."

I went into the hospital each time prepared to tell my newborn those words, but it turned out I was the one who needed to hear them. I needed the reminder, "Do I know who I am? I'm the one Jesus loves." I needed, in that moment, to live in that truth and to be shaped by my identity.

Perhaps you've had an alias. You've been given other names besides your real one. Could it be that those names have shaped you? Maybe they've left you feeling unlovable, unable to understand how you could possibly be the one Jesus loves.

Well, other people may have told you that you're not worth much, but the truth is that God wouldn't trade you for anything. In fact, when he set the price tag on you, it was his Son.

And you may be torn and broken. You may still bear the marks of deep wounds. But God is a master at reconstructive surgery.

And perhaps, because of all this, you have difficulty connecting with God. You feel like your prayers bounce back at you off the ceiling. At church other people sing out the worship songs, but you struggle to, not necessarily because you have a bad voice but because the words come from a bad heart. And so you're sure that to God, it's bad music. But no, when God hears you, he moves in tight.

You know why? Because you are his. Because since the beginning of your life, you have belonged to him. He shaped you in your mother's womb and his finger marks are permanently embedded in you.

You are the one Jesus loves.

HUNGRY

6

Why don't I live life with Jesus? What holds me back from abiding? It's not just the names that have shaped me; I think it also has something to do with being hungry.

One time Jesus was surrounded by thousands of hungry people who had no food, so he did a miracle and fed the entire group with some kid's Happy Meal. The next morning everyone is back, and why not? They found someone who provides a free meal, and they're hungry again. But Jesus refuses to give them breakfast. Instead he tells them, "Do not work for food that spoils, but for food that endures to eternal life."[1]

The people in the crowd are like, "What? We don't understand the words that are coming out of your mouth. What are you saying? We are hungry for bread. Give us some bread!"

Jesus responds, "I am the bread of life. He who comes to me will never go hungry."[2]

The crowd is confused, "What? You speak in riddles. Can you be clearer?"

Jesus says, "Unless you eat my flesh and drink my blood, you have no life in you."[3]

The people are like, "Okay, it sounds like he wants us to eat his flesh and drink his blood. Jesus, I don't think you realize what you just said."

Jesus replies, "Whoever eats my flesh and drinks my blood has eternal life."[4]

Crowd: "Did we just hear him right?"

Jesus: "For my flesh is real food and my blood is real drink."[5]

Crowd: "I dare you to say that one more time."

Jesus: "Whoever eats my flesh and drinks my blood remains in me, and I in him."[6]

The Bible tells us this was the day almost everyone decided not to follow Jesus anymore.

I bet this was also the day when Jesus' closest disciples realized they had a problem: Jesus was a loose cannon. I can picture them, later that night, suggesting to Jesus that perhaps they could help him with his PR.

"Now Jesus, if we heard you correctly, earlier, your new marketing slogan is:

Bite Me!

"No offense, pal, but we're not feeling that. Some of us were talking and we came up with a few new ideas that might do some damage control. What about these slogans?

Flesh and Blood? C'mon, Can't You Guys Take a Joke?

or

Call Me What You Want . . . Just Don't Call Me Dinner

or

Full Bellies for Everyone—And Not from Eating Jesus!

or

Christianity: Our Leader Is Really Committed to His Metaphors!

And Jesus would have smiled and been like, "No thanks, dudes."

And his disciples would respond, "Okay, yeah, we figured that. So here's another idea. What if we use humor? You know, lighten things up by having some fun with this whole controversy deal. That could win some people back. So check it out. The next time you preach you could start with this:

> Good evening, ladies and gentlemen . . . So, speaking of eating my flesh and drinking my blood . . . What did the cannibal get when he was late for dinner? . . . The cold shoulder.

"Wait, why aren't you laughing, Jesus? Don't you get it? The cold *shoulder*. Okay, well what about this?

> So I went to a restaurant the other day and their sign said, "Breakfast at any time," so I ordered French Toast during the Renaissance.[7]

"C'mon, Jesus, that's hysterical! The Renaissance hasn't even happened yet. You can be funny, and a prophet, at the same time!"

Jesus would've answered, "I'll think about it, but for now I'm sticking with what I've got."

Jesus knew that people are hungry and want something that will satisfy them. He also knew that only God truly satisfies. So he just wouldn't budge off the "I'm the thing you have to eat" line.

I've been trying to figure this out, and I think maybe my problem is that *I have a roving appetite*. Jesus said *he* needs to be what I'm hungry for, but it's as if I go around in life with a fork in my hand, stabbing at anything that looks like it might taste good or stave off my hunger pains.

This started when I was very young. As a child I became convinced that what was missing from my life were Star Wars action figures, so I stabbed at that. Then it was an Atari game system, then dating this girl at school, then making the all-star team, then getting my driver's license, then owning a car, then moving out of the house, then getting a job, then getting a better car, then finding a wife, then owning a house, then having a child. I've spent my life stabbing at anything that moved, sure that something would fill me up. But after eating all this stuff I always end up hungry.

And I can still be this way. Lately the thing I'm stabbing at is church "growth." As a pastor, I assume that if my church grew to a certain size, I would be satisfied. So I spend half my time and most of my energy trying to figure out how to grow my church. I try everything, but still our church doesn't grow to my satisfaction. I start to wonder if there's some secret that pastors of megachurches are in on but are keeping from me.

One day I saw a trailer for a movie called *The Sisterhood of the Traveling Pants*. It's about four teenage girls who are about to be separated for the summer. These four best friends find a pair of pants that, though the four are different shapes and sizes, amazingly fits each of them. They decide to use the "magic" pants to keep in touch over the summer. They send the pants around and each girl must wear them to receive the good luck they bring. I realized this could be it! Maybe the secret covert club of megachurch pastors is "The Brotherhood of the Traveling Underpants." Rick Warren and Bill Hybels and T. D. Jakes and all those guys found a magical pair of boxers and have been passing them around, bringing phenomenal church growth to whoever is wearing them at the moment. I have to get my hands on their underpants!

Seriously, this roving appetite thing is everywhere. I know women who have romance fantasies about almost every guy except their husbands, while their husbands have sex fantasies about almost every girl except their wives. I know parents who so desperately need for their kids to succeed in life they'll do anything, including making their kids miserable. I know kids who so desperately need their parent's approval, they'll do anything, including making themselves miserable. I know rock stars who wish they did something meaningful, and worship leaders who wish they were rock stars. I know teenagers who are alone and would do anything to become popular so they could be surrounded by friends, and I know popular kids who can't stop feeling alone even when they are surrounded by friends. I know poor people who wish they had more so they could escape the pressures of their poverty, and I know rich people who wish they had less so they could escape the pressures of their possessions.

We have roving appetites, so we go around stabbing and eating anything and everything we can, but nothing seems to satisfy.

A couple of years ago I went to Laos on a mission trip and to see my friend Mark. Mark is one of two friends I have who are six-foot-five. That's just greedy. Mark and I are really good friends. On one occasion, his cousin died and he had to drive to Ohio for the funeral. He was going alone, so I offered to join him. The best thing that happened on that trip is that we went through a drive-thru, and Mark asked for "extra mustard" on his hamburger. Five minutes later we were driving down the highway when Mark growled, "Very funny!"

"What's very funny?" I asked. Then I looked and saw mustard everywhere. It looked like a mustard bomb had just gone off. Peering through the mustard, I could see Mark was angry.

"This is his idea of extra mustard, huh? Very funny." You have to love a guy who dares to order extra mustard.

So I was excited to see Mark in Laos. But when I did, I barely recognized him. "Is that you?" I asked.

"Very funny," Mark said. "You don't recognize me without the mustard coating?" Mark has a hard time letting go of things.

But it wasn't that Mark was no longer in the Yellow Man Group, it was that he had lost about forty pounds, and it had only been about six months. "Dude," I screamed, "you've got to eat!"

Mark explained that he *was* eating, more than ever. He was always hungry and ate nonstop. He said maybe the weight loss was a result of eating healthier foods. I told him he was nuts—there was no way he'd lose forty pounds that fast just by eating healthier.

And it turned out I was right. Mark later discovered that he had worms. Somehow worms had gotten in his system and they were devouring everything Mark ate. This left him always empty, always hungry, always eating, but never feeling satisfied.

Sometimes I feel like that. I'm always empty, always hungry, always eating, but never full. My whole life I've been stabbing at stuff nonstop, but somehow it hasn't satisfied me.

I also wonder if I'm not *really* hungry. Jesus used hunger as a metaphor for how we're to feel about God, but

I have no real experience with being truly hungry for food. And so I can't understand what he meant.

I have, however, been hungry for *sleep*.

On that trip to Laos I slept almost never. It started with a twenty-two-hour flight, and I just can't sleep on airplanes. We had a ten-hour layover in Thailand. I tried to sleep on the floor of the airport, but it wasn't happening. The first few nights in Laos, my body was adjusting to the thirteen-hour time difference. I was so tired I would fall asleep immediately, but three hours later I'd be wide awake. Then we traveled to a different town where we stayed in a five-dollar hotel for two nights. My bed was a board. It was awful, and I barely slept at all. But that hotel was like the Ritz-Carlton compared to what I experienced the following night.

We traveled in a truck to a rural, tiny speck of a Lao village. The hotel there was horrible. Like the-inside-of-a-raccoon's-intestine horrible. One guy on our team described it this way: "Picture the most disgusting, filthiest, sickest gas station bathroom you've ever seen . . . now picture sleeping in it." Dirty mosquito nets dangled from the ceiling, rats were scurrying around, there were red footprints going *up* the wall! (Why *red* and why *up the walls* I have no idea.) There was one bathroom for the entire hotel. It had a hole in the floor, a tub full of putrid water, and that's it.

The owner was a young Chinese lady who spoke neither Lao nor English, so we couldn't communicate with her. Our host in Laos asked a woman walking by, "Why does a Chinese woman own a hotel here in Laos?" She said, "Oh, she come here to start business. She sell you room . . . and her body."

We were like, "Great. We've traveled across the world to stay at the worst little whorehouse in Laos!"

That night all the lights suddenly went out. We learned that at 9:00 p.m. the town generator is turned off and all the power goes down. We each grabbed our flashlights and went to bed. I refused to touch my bed so I put an inflatable mattress on top of it. I placed my suitcase next to my bed and my watch on top of my suitcase, because I knew I wouldn't be sleeping and I'd want to check what time it was all night.

A couple of minutes later I heard a plastic bag rustling. I thought the guy sharing my room was trying to be funny, so I said, "Stop it, Chris," but he swore it wasn't him. Then I realized we had left a bag of cookies on the floor. I turned on my flashlight and saw that the bag had been moved across the room. The cookies were all over. I *freaked* out. I hastily collected all the food, put it back in the bag, cracked open our door and yelled, "Skanky . . ." (that's what I had named the rat, on account of his choosing to live in a whorehouse). "Skanky, this food is our offering to you. We give it to you now on the condition that you stay out here and eat it. Don't come back in our room!" Then I chucked it out in the hall, slammed the door, and sprinted back to my bed like a four-year-old being chased by the boogeyman.

A minute later we were lying in the dark when I again heard the sound of a plastic bag rustling. I said, "Oh, that's hysterical, Chris!"

"It's not me," he answered.

"Oh no, the potato chips!" I hollered.

I pointed my flashlight at the bag on the table . . . and I found myself staring directly into the eyes of the beast. Skanky looked right at me, jumped off the table, onto my suitcase, and ran straight at my face.

I screamed.

A guy on our team who was in a room upstairs came bolting down, ran into our room and yelled, "Who was that?"

I raised my hand.

"Oh." He looked confused. "I thought it was a girl."

I tried to go to sleep but soon there was yelling from upstairs. Two ladies from our team were wigging out because a rat was in their room. They marched downstairs and announced, "We are *not* sleeping in this place."

"You said it, sister!" I shouted in agreement.

Chris explained that there was nothing the rats could do to us, and we should just calm down and get back in our beds. But us girls weren't having it. We decided to go out and sleep in the truck.

That was when we discovered that the owner of the place had padlocked the front door. The lock was intended to keep people from coming *in*, but it was keeping us from going *out*. We would have asked the owner to unlock it, but the noises coming from her room indicated we weren't the only customers requiring her attention at the moment. So we started searching for a way out. Finally, we found an open window. We had to climb up to it, squeeze through, and then free fall to the ground. We then spent the rest of the night in the back of the pickup truck. Once again, I didn't sleep at all.

It had now been over a week since we left home, and I had only slept parts of maybe four or five nights. I was dragging myself around zombie-like during the day, barely making it, jonesing for even a second of shut-eye.

During that trip I knew what it meant to be hungry, *really hungry*—not for food but for sleep.

And I think that's the kind of hunger Jesus is talking about. But perhaps my problem is that I'm not hungry for God like I was in Laos for sleep. My hunger for God isn't a total desperation for him, but *that's* what I need.

⟡

Or maybe part of the reason I don't live life with Jesus and instead lapse into spiritual starvation is because

I think that being hungry for God will automatically lead to being filled with God. I think that *wanting it* is enough. And I hear this from almost every Christian I talk to. They say, "I *want* so badly to grow spiritually, but it's just not happening. I don't get it. It's so frustrating." Or "I don't understand. I don't *want* to give in to this temptation anymore, so why do I keep doing it?" Or "It doesn't make sense, I *want* to be closer to God, so why aren't I?"

We assume that wanting it is enough, that being hungry for God will automatically lead to being filled with God. But the more I think about that, the more I realize how strange an idea this really is. I mean, we can't just *want* to be in good shape physically and it automatically just happens. We can't just *want* to get good grades in school and it automatically just happens. We can't just *want* to have a great relationship with our spouse and it automatically just happens. Everything important in life takes some work, some discipline, so why should it be any different with God? Yes, we need to want it, we need to be hungry. But being hungry is not enough. The people listening to Jesus back then knew that. Going from hungry to full was not automatic for them like it is for us. They knew that to go from hungry to full they would need to take the appropriate steps; they would have to create the right conditions for eating. Whether it was hunting for berries or bison, baking bread, or butchering a billy goat, a variety of things had to happen before they could say, "Wow, now that was a great meal."

Because eating is so easy for us, I think we once more need a different metaphor. And, again, the one that works for me is sleep.

If you've stared at the ceiling like me, you've reached a point where you want to fall asleep badly. I've had nights where I've insisted, "That's it! I'm not fooling around

anymore. I'm going to fall asleep right now! Right . . . now!
. . . Crap! Okay, I have to get up in six hours. Seriously,
I am going to fall asleep . . . right . . . now! Okay, now I
have to get up in five hours and forty-five minutes. I mean
it this time, I am going to fall asleep right . . . now!" But
does wanting to fall asleep badly help me fall asleep? No.
In fact, sometimes it hurts my ability to fall asleep.

So, what *helps* a person to fall asleep? The only thing
that helps is taking the steps to create the right conditions in which to fall asleep. We are supposed to fall
asleep naturally, and the only thing we can do to help
the process is to create the right conditions for falling
asleep.

I have a really hard time falling asleep, which forced
me to become an expert at creating the right conditions
for doing so.

I need the room pitch black. When I sleep in a hotel,
I bring duct tape to get the curtains to totally cover the
windows. Pitch black is a necessity.

I also need the room totally silent. Some like music
or white noise. I require silence.

Most people use one pillow, I require two. Here's why:
The top of my head must be at least one degree higher
than the rest of my head. If my head is flat or tilted down
I feel like blood is rushing to the top. It's like trying to fall
asleep on a rollercoaster! So I strategically position my
two pillows so that my head is at just the right angle.

I have a sheet that covers me all the way to my shoulders, but the blanket on top of it must only cover my
legs.

So we need to be hungry for sleep *and* we must create
the right conditions for falling asleep.

But those of us who do actually get hungry for God
think it's enough, and so we do nothing to create the
right conditions to go from being hungry for God to
being filled with God.

We're like a person in Jesus' day who is hungry, but going from hungry to filled would mean walking to the vineyard to pick some grapes, or going fishing and then cleaning and cooking the fish. And this person is not willing, or too lazy, or just has other things he wants to do, and so eventually he starves to death.

That would obviously be ridiculous, but I wonder sometimes if it describes my spiritual life. I'm hungry for God, but going from being hungry to being full would take blocking out some time and really spending it with him reading my Bible, or maybe it would take getting into a small group at church, or reading a book about prayer. And I'm not willing, or I'm lazy, or it's just that I have a lot of other things to do, and so I'm starving spiritually. I'm disappointed with my Christian life, and I'm blaming it on God.

Or perhaps my biggest problem is that I don't stay hungry for God. I've had times in my life when I realized that my hunger was a spiritual hunger, and I became desperate for God, and I looked to him alone, and I created the right conditions to be filled by him, and I had this strange experience of actually feeling full, of having my hunger sated. And I lived life with Jesus and it was amazing.

The problem is that it didn't last. My roving appetite came back to bite me, or my hunger became complacent, or I started assuming that being filled by God just happens by itself, so I stopped taking the necessary steps to create the right conditions. And then I found myself confused and wondering what I was missing. And so maybe my real problem is that I don't stay hungry for God.

Earlier I mentioned Mark. My other friend who is six-foot-five is Toby. Toby went to my church for several years while he was in college and also did an internship on our church staff for two years. During his internship Toby had two cars. Both of those cars caught on fire.

One morning Toby walked into our office, sat down at his desk, and began working. A few minutes later he realized he had left some papers in his car. When he went back out into the parking lot, it looked like a scene from the movie *Backdraft*. It startled him, but Toby's bright, and he wears glasses, so he quickly realized someone's car was on fire. Then Toby realized it was *his* car on fire.

That just was not cool.

A few months later Toby was driving on the highway when the guy in the car next to him started beeping and waving. Toby beeped and waved back. The guy continued beeping and waving. This time Toby did not respond in kind. But the other guy wouldn't give up. He rolled down his window. Toby rolled down his window, but he's from New York, so he was muttering about how people in the South are too friendly. The guy screamed, "Fire!" Toby said, "What?" This guy screamed, "Your car is on fire!"

That also was not cool.

I am fascinated by the idea that one person could have two cars catch fire in the same year—not to mention determining the mathematical improbability of that—but this is not why I have to tell you about Toby. I have to tell you about Toby because of his trip to Africa.

While he was there he went on safari in a game preserve in Kenya. The group spotted a lion up on a hill. They asked the safari guide, a Kenyan native, if lions ever kill people. The guide said, "It happens rarely, but if one does, the lion won't last very long."

Someone asked him, "What do you mean? Why don't they last long?"

"Once a lion kills a human," the guide answered, "everyone in the area joins together to hunt him. Because once he has a taste for human blood, he will kill again and again and again. He is hungry for man and he will not stop until he dies."

I want to have a taste for the flesh and blood of Jesus. I want a hunger that doesn't quit.

So how? How do I stay hungry for God?

If you're like me and have a roving appetite and a bunch of other problems, how can you stay hungry for God?

The other day a guy from my church called and asked if we could get together at a coffee shop. He's been struggling for a while in all kinds of ways. He hasn't even shown his face in church lately.

With tears in his eyes he told me how bad his life had gotten. I said, "Jay, I think you know what you need. You need God. You need to be hungry for God."

He started to look frustrated and said, "I know, Vince. But the problem is I don't want God. I used to be so excited about him, about praying, reading the Bible, going to church, all of it. But somehow I've drifted away, and I just don't care. I'm not hungry for God anymore, and I have no idea how to get that back."

I was quiet for a long time. We just kind of looked at each other and listened to the occasional noise from the coffee grinder. And then, finally, I said, "All right, Jay, I've got two ideas. Maybe they could help.

"The first one is that you need to eat, even if you're not hungry. I read somewhere that if a person doesn't eat for long enough, they stop feeling hungry. This person could be starving to death, but still they don't feel hungry. At some point they completely lose interest in food. Typically people eat because they're hungry, but for this person who is literally starving, eating is the only thing that will induce hunger.

"Maybe it's been so long since you've really connected with God that you don't feel hungry for him at all. You're just not interested. And perhaps the only thing that will induce the hunger you need is eating. And so, even if you don't feel hungry for God, could you force yourself to eat? Maybe sit down and read the Bible today. Or pray. Or go back to your small group tomorrow night. Or come to church on Sunday. Or just sit in silence and beg God to speak to you.

"And that leads into my other idea. Maybe rather than you trying to make yourself hungry for God, maybe you should ask God to make you hungry for God.

"When my son was three years old he was the cutest kid in the world. And he had this thing he would say about twenty times a day. He'd look up at me and say, 'Daddeee, I'm hungeee.' Jay, have you ever heard a ridiculously cute three-year-old say, 'Daddeee, I'm hungeee'? I'll tell you what: if the only food to be had was four thousand miles away, and I had to do a naked crawl over broken glass to get it, I would. He's my kid, I love him; how could I say no?

"I think God is the same way. If you look up at him with big eyes and say, 'Daddeee, I'm hungeee,' or even, 'Daddeee, I'm not hungeee, please make me hungeee,' I bet his heart melts. And he just has to respond to that cry."

FOLLOW

7

I don't think people who lived in the Bible times had it easy, but at least when Jesus said, "Follow me," they could see the guy. You knew whether you were following him or not because . . . "Whoa, there goes Jesus!" He'd be off somewhere and you'd still be eating your cheese fries (because chili cheese fries hadn't been invented yet—man, they had it rough) and you'd realize, "Whoops, I guess I didn't follow."

I think in many ways those of us who live today have it easier, but following an invisible guy can be tricky. When I wanted to start doing it, I realized I didn't even know what it meant.

My first image of "following Jesus" portrayed him steadily walking a straight, narrow path with a Christian dutifully trailing behind, trying to never get distracted and led off course. Most of the people I talked to seemed to hold this view.

But after a while I realized that with this way of thinking, Jesus is almost completely irrelevant to following

Jesus. This concerned me. If all a Christian has to do is stay on the straight and narrow path of obedience by doing right and not doing wrong, does it really matter if Jesus is out in front or not?

In fact, Jesus could faint; I could walk right past him and still feel assured that I'm "following Jesus," because I've stayed on that same straight, moral path. Jesus could then wake up and start walking the same course again, only now he'd be following me! There had to be something wrong with my understanding of following Jesus if it didn't really matter who was following who.

This view of following Jesus is captured in an old saying (and someone wrote a book with this title) about how the Christian life is "a long obedience in the same direction."[1] Now don't get me wrong, I know there is truth in that. Being a Christian *does* involve obeying God over the long haul. And part of following Jesus *is* doing right and not doing wrong. But there's got to be more to it.

I decided to look at the original followers of Jesus in the Bible. I was still a little annoyed with them, because they had the advantage of getting the noninvisible Jesus, but I hoped maybe I could learn something. What did it look like for them to follow Jesus?

Did following Jesus lead them to obedience and morality? Yes.

But was it more than that? Way more.

It's wacky. People are following Jesus into a storm your momma would have made you come in from. People are giving up everything and leaving their jobs to follow Jesus. Jesus speaks of those who follow him as having the light of life, and being able to hear and recognize his voice, so they'd know which way to go. Jesus says that to follow is to serve. Followers claim crazy things like "Let me follow, I'll lay down my life for you" and "Let's follow Jesus to our deaths!"[2] People stop following

Jesus in droves because it's too weird or too scary, or he offends them by saying they need to eat him. Mark 10:32 reports: "They were on their way up to Jerusalem, with Jesus leading the way, and the disciples were astonished, while those who followed were afraid." Everywhere I looked, it seemed like following Jesus led people to be astonished and afraid.

Following Jesus did not lead people in one monotonous direction; it led them in all different directions. Jesus was constantly on the move. He had an agenda. And following him meant you would be going where he was going and doing what he was doing.

Following Jesus is a long obedience in all different directions.

I coached my son's soccer team for three years. These were teams of three- and then four- and then five-year-olds. One of the drills we did at practice is called "Catch the Coach." All the kids were in a pack and each had a soccer ball. I yelled, "Go!" and then started running. They'd have to follow and catch me as they dribbled their soccer balls. So I'd be running to the right, and they'd all be following along pretty well, then I'd cut hard to the left. Those with better ball handling skills would cut with me and stay close behind. Other kids would still be going in the wrong direction, wondering where their team went. Eventually they'd make a big wide turn and finally they'd go in the correct direction again, but they'd be way behind me. Then I'd stop and start running right at the kids. The better players would stop, turn around, and stay right with me. The less advanced players continued in their same direction. They tended to end up in the parking lot, dodging minivans.

That soccer drill is my new image of following Jesus. Being a Christian is not so much about dutifully checking off a list of expected behaviors I'm supposed to do (and not do) each day so I stay on the long walk of obedience in the same direction. It's about following Jesus *wherever* he goes. It's about watching him closely, learning how he moves, anticipating what he might do next, and keeping the space between him and me as small (and decreasing) as possible.

I'm no expert at this, but I'm getting better. Because he's invisible and all, I'm often not positive I'm following Jesus, but I've been asking God to help me. I keep telling him I want to follow Jesus wherever he leads, even if I'm astonished at where he wants to take me and afraid of going there.

Here's an example: A few years ago my wife and I were looking for a house to buy. My wife fell in love with one, and eventually we went to sign the contract. At the desk, with the papers in front of us, I started feeling sick. I had this overwhelming sense that we shouldn't buy the house. I asked Jen if I could speak to her outside and we left the real estate agents inside. I explained that I knew it was freaky and all, but I had this sense that Jesus was leading us to not buy this house. She was angry. "Are you *sure* it was Jesus?"

I said, "Of course not, the dude's invisible!"

She was angrier. She asked, "Well then, what—did you hear his voice or something?"

I said, "Well, you know, I mean, umm, I think his voice is invisible too . . ."

She asked, "So, we're *really* not going to buy this house? What about the real estate agents sitting inside waiting for their commission? What do we say to them?"

I yelled, "Whoa, there goes Jesus!" and ran to the car.

Looking back now, five years later, sitting in the house we ended up buying, it is *totally* obvious that purchasing the other house would have been a mistake. It wouldn't have been immoral. I could have completely stayed on the moral path and bought that house, but I wouldn't have been following Jesus.

⌒

Another time I was at my office talking to my wife on the phone. She asked, "What are you doing for lunch?"

I answered, "Going to CiCi's." In case you don't know, CiCi's is an all-you-can-eat pizza buffet. The pizza is average, but the desserts are good, and the cinnamon rolls are worth killing your grandma for.

She asked, "Who are you going with?"

"By myself," I answered.

"Why?" she asked.

I could hear an incredulous tone in her voice and so, wanting to defend myself, I explained, "I'm going to bring my laptop and work there this afternoon."

"You're going to what?"

"I'm going to bring my laptop and work there this afternoon."

"You're going to an all-you-can-eat pizza buffet . . . for the *entire* afternoon?" Her voice was getting louder. "Are you planning on *eating* the entire afternoon?"

"Yes," I replied. (I had thought she would admire the financial wisdom of planning to spend an entire day at an all-you-can-eat restaurant, but now I wasn't sure.)

"You can't do that. They won't allow it."

I could not believe she went there. Implying that I wallowed in the sin of gluttony was expected, but questioning my understanding of the all-you-can-eat buffet? I don't think so! "Of course you're *allowed* to do that. It's not all-you-can-eat-in-an-hour, it's all-you-can-eat . . . period."

"Well," she answered, "even if they let you, don't you think there's something wrong with you sitting there and eating pizza all day?"

Ahh, that was better. She had brought it around to gluttony. I was no longer insulted. My anger subsided. I told her, "I think I'm supposed to go."

"What do you mean you're *supposed* to go?"

"I don't know why," I explained, "but all day I've felt like I'm kind of supposed to go to CiCi's and be there."

"It's just because you want to eat pizza and cinnamon rolls all day today."

"No," I countered, "I want to eat pizza and cinnamon rolls all day *every day*, but I never have. But I am going to today."

So I went. As I sat at the table working and eating my eighty-second cinnamon roll, I noticed this girl checking me out. Now being devastatingly handsome and drop-dead sexy, I wouldn't be surprised if you would assume I'd have girls checking me out all the time, but I don't. So this girl checking me out surprised me. I thought, *Yep . . . I've still got it* as I tried to wipe off the cinnamon roll icing that was stuck in my eyebrow. Then the girl started walking over toward me. I thought, *Poor thing, she's going to be devastated when she hears that I'm married* as I blotted some of the big pizza stain off my shirt. She stopped at my table and said, "Do I know you?"

A variety of possible responses went through my head: I could (1) scream, "I'm married! Why are you trying to break up my family?" (2) use my old reliable line from my single days: "Did you used to be larvae? Because, girl, you are so fly!" or (3) feign a cinnamon roll–induced heart attack.

Instead I said, "No."

She asked, "Are you sure?"

"Well, have you ever been to Forefront Church?" I asked. "If so, you would have seen me speak there."

"No," she said. "I don't go to church. Well, I used to, but that was a long time ago. I've been thinking that I should go, though. See, my husband just left me. So my daughter and I moved back here to Virginia Beach . . . this is where I grew up. Anyway, I could swear I know you."

"Nope," I mumbled (my mouth full of cinnamon roll).

"Well," she seemed confused, "please don't think I'm weird, but the whole time I've been here I've felt like I was supposed to come and talk to you. I thought maybe it was because I knew you. I don't get it. Why do you think I felt like I'm supposed to come over and talk to you?"

"Well, please don't think *I'm* weird," I answered, "but do you think it's possible that it was God? If you've been thinking that you and your daughter need to go back to church, and then you feel like you're supposed to talk to this guy, who happens to be a pastor . . ."

And we proceeded to have a very cool conversation. And why did all that happen? I think it was because somehow I was listening for the voice of Jesus, and he led me to CiCi's. I don't think *not* going to CiCi's would have been immoral. In fact, I can make a good argument that not going to CiCi's would have made me *more* moral, but I wouldn't have been following Jesus.

Unfortunately, not understanding what it meant to follow Jesus wasn't my only problem. I also wasn't sure I'd like where he would lead me. I mean, it's cool when it's CiCi's, but that's not usually the way Jesus rolls.

The deal is that God hasn't changed much. Let me explain what I mean.

What is the first thing we see God doing in the Bible? I think the correct answer is "hovering." The Bible describes what God was hovering over as "formless," "empty," and "darkness."[3] It's like God was hovering over this dark, chaotic messiness. What happens next? God dives into it, and he brings light to the darkness, order to the chaos, and beauty to the messiness.

When I study the life of Jesus, I see this happening all the time. Jesus' MO was to go into a town, hover around a little, and then dive into the dark, chaotic, messy places in people's lives and bring light, order, and beauty. He went into Samaria, hovered a little, then dove into the dark, chaotic messiness of a woman who was changing husbands almost as often as I change underwear. Jesus brought light, order, and beauty to her life. He went into Jericho, hovered a little, then dove into the dark, chaotic messiness of a short runt of a man who embezzled people's money through his position as chief tax collector. Jesus brought light, order, and beauty to his life. He went into Jerusalem, hovered a little, then dove into the dark, chaotic messiness of a man who had been paralyzed for thirty-eight years, unable to get into a pool that allegedly brought healing and thus was instead wallowing in a pool of self-pity. Jesus brought light, order, and beauty to his life.[4]

See, God hasn't changed much. What we find him doing at the beginning of the Old Testament we find him doing in the beginning of the New Testament. And he's still doing the same thing today.

So what I've come to realize is that if I follow Jesus, he may let me hover with him for a little while, but then he always leads me to bring light to darkness, order to chaos, and beauty to messiness.

Sometimes Jesus will lead me into the darkness, chaos, and messiness of *my own life*. Though I prefer to ignore it, the reality is that wherever there is sin in my life, there is darkness, chaos, and messiness. This is part of the reason so many Christians wear a disappointed look on their faces. The fully alive life of following Jesus is one marked by light, order and beauty, but our lives often remain anything but. We blame God for this and question why he hasn't lived up to the promises he gives us in the Bible, but *he's* not the problem. If we were following Jesus, he would lead us into the darkness of our sin so we would deal with it and see that area of our life transformed, but we're not really following him.

One time a guy in my small group announced rather loudly, "My life was better *before* I became a Christian." Everyone kind of gasped, but I said, "Of course it was." This led to a second gasp. In the past, this guy had been honest with our group, and we all knew that he had a pattern of sin he was unwilling to give up. I said to him, "Before you became a Christian, because of your sin, your life was dark, chaotic, and messy. It wasn't good, but for you it was normal. Since you've become a Christian, you *still* have that same sin in your life, and so your life is *still* the same. The difference now is that you have Jesus in your life, trying to lead you into the chaos of that sin, to deal with it; to understand what's causing it, why you feel like you need it, and to let it go. He loves you, so he won't give up on you, and he's continually trying to lead you in that direction. But you're continually struggling against him. So now your life is dark, chaotic, and messy, *and* you have this constant struggle against Jesus. So *of course* your life was better before you became a Christian."

Then I asked if anyone had tried CiCi's cinnamon rolls, because, yummy, they're good.

I hope I don't sound like I'm judging that guy, because I'm not. In fact, I'm just like him. For years I continued in the sin of being an impatient jerk to people. The whole time Jesus was trying to lead me into the messiness of that sin, but I didn't want to go there. I didn't want to deal with my past, with what my father had done to me, with what I had become. I didn't want to get the help I needed. And so I struggled against Jesus until the pain of being a disappointed, toxic Christian became greater than the fear of following him.

Although it seems easier to just continue hovering, I'm learning it's always better to follow Jesus as he dives into the dark, chaotic, messiness of my sin. It's usually scary, but it always leads me to light, order, and beauty. And it's the only way to really experience life with Jesus.

Sometimes Jesus will lead me into the darkness, chaos, and messiness in my own life, but other times Jesus leads me into the darkness, chaos, and messiness in *other* people's lives. And I *never* want to go there. But, again, it's the only way I can follow Jesus.

One time I was standing in the lobby after a Sunday morning church service when a couple I had never seen before walked up. I said, "Hey! Is this your first time here?"

They both smiled and she said, "Yes."

He immediately chimed in, "We *loved* it!"

"Yeah," she added, "we didn't know church could be like this. It was great."

"We have a question for you," he said, "but first, I'm John, and this is Michelle."

"Nice to meet you. I'm Vince."

"So anyway," he continued, "here's our question. We're both bisexuals, and when we got married, I promised Michelle I wouldn't sleep with any more *women*."

"And I promised John I wouldn't sleep with any more *men*," Michelle added, right on cue.

"But we still both sleep with people of the same sex," John continued. "That's okay, right?"

A variety of possible responses went through my head: I could (1) scream, "Okay, I'm being punk'd! Where are you, Ashton Kutcher? Show me the hidden camera!" (2) use my old reliable line, "Sorry, they didn't teach us about this in seminary," or (3) feign a cinnamon roll–induced heart attack.

Instead, I said, "That's a really good question. Would you want to get together some time and talk about it?"

They said sure, smiled, shook my hand, and left. As they walked away, I thought, *Why do I have to deal with this? It's personal. It's their business, not mine. I don't want to make them mad. Why do I have to deal with this?* And then I realized: it's because I'm following Jesus, and God has never really changed much. If Jesus were here, he'd hover around in the lobby a little, and then dive into the dark, chaotic messiness of that bisexual couple's life and he would bring light, order, and beauty. So, if I'm following Jesus, *of course* that's where he'll lead me.

Pretty soon I was meeting with that couple, trying to explain that God loved them, and that his primary concern was not to get them to stop sinning but to experience his love. Once they experienced his love, it should lead them to stop sinning. And then their lives would be marked by light, and order, and beauty, in places now dominated by darkness, chaos, and messiness. Surprisingly, they weren't mad. They were curious. They wanted to talk more. Eventually they wanted to change. They struggled. They fell back into old sin patterns. They asked for accountability. Michelle requested that my wife and I drive by her favorite gay bar every Saturday night to make sure her car was not in the parking lot. If it was, she said, please come in and drag her out. That was not a place I was excited for Jesus to lead me into.

In many ways following Jesus in this couple's lives led my wife and me into darkness, chaos, and messiness. And we didn't want to do it. But we did. And we learned that although it seems easier to just hover in the lobby, it's always better to follow Jesus, even as he dives into the sin of other people's lives.

⌒

If you're disappointed, is it possible you're not really living life with Jesus, because you're not really following him? He's gone somewhere, you haven't followed, and so now, you're somewhere else.

And I understand that it's daunting to think about— this idea of following Jesus wherever he wants to go and of being led into dark, chaotic, messy places you'd prefer to stay away from.

At least it is for me.

But I'm discovering that Jesus is trustworthy, and that wherever he wants me, it's probably the best place for me.

And I've had to ask myself: *Has my way of doing life really worked that well?*

How about you? Aren't you reading this book because you feel like something has been missing from your life, like something is missing from your Christian experience?

Maybe it's time to start really following Jesus.

Go catch the invisible guy.

GLOW

8

A few years ago my wife and I became T-shirt wearers—"I Got Married and All I Got Was This Lousy T-Shirt." Well, we didn't actually have them made up, but we might as well have.

When we first started dating and got married, we had something special. Other people were annoyed because we only wanted to be with each other. We never got tired of each other. After work we would play tennis, go out to eat, play Yahtzee, and talk for hours—almost every single night. On weekends it was more of the same. After we got married people would ask, "Are you two making sure you have a date night? You have to have a weekly date night!" and we'd laugh behind their backs. We had a date *life*.

Then something happened. Maybe it was our familiarity with each other or increased work demands, or having kids and all the responsibilities that brings. I'm not sure why, but our relationship changed. The intimacy was dwindling. The sense of adventure we once had was being snuffed out by a passionless daily routine. It was all just . . . disappointing.

After a few years, we realized it wasn't going to "just get better" and that we didn't want to feel stuck for the rest of our lives. My wife told me we needed counseling.

The counselor had us describe our relationship. We told him that we were both pretty busy. We were together a lot, like in the house at night, but each doing our own thing. And we were in the car together a lot, like driving the kids to their activities, but we didn't talk much, or really do anything truly *together*.

The counselor had us describe what our relationship *used* to look like. We told him about our old date life. (We had a PowerPoint presentation including several pictures of daisies, one of me covered in body glitter playing dodgeball, and two embarrassing shots of Jen and me together in a bathtub full of rice pudding.)

The counselor told us we needed to start doing what we used to do.

"What we *used* to do?" we asked.

"Yeah," the counselor explained, "play tennis, go out to eat, play Yahtzee, talk for hours. Have a date life again."

"But why would we do *that*?" we asked.

"Because that's what you did when things were going great. Don't you think maybe the problem is that you stopped?" he asked. "So rearrange your schedules, reduce your responsibilities, and make whatever changes you have to so that you can start spending large quantities of quality time together—face-to-face. It needs to be face-to-face."

We tentatively decided to give it a shot. I committed to stop bringing my laptop home from work. Jen promised she'd get her stuff done during the day.

And so the next night we sat down face-to-face for the first time in a while. "What the crap are we supposed to talk about?" I asked.

"I have no idea," Jen answered.

"Maybe we shouldn't jump right into talking. Is there something a little easier we could start with?" I wondered out loud.

"Yahtzee!" we both screamed.

We started spending quality time together each evening, we committed to a weekly date night, and we tried to plan a short getaway each year. We focused on things that would bring us face-to-face.

And things started changing. It was awkward at first, but then it gradually gained momentum and soon, the T-shirts were removed.

⌒

There's a guy in the Old Testament who became a T-shirt wearer—"I Was Chosen by God, Led His People Out of Slavery and Through the Red Sea, and All I Got Was This Lousy T-Shirt." Well, he didn't actually have the T-shirt made up . . . instead, he wore a veil.

Moses was this guy who had murdered some dude and stuttered like P-P-P-Porky Pig, but God still chose him to be the leader of his people. Moses would represent God's people before God, and he'd represent God before his people. Moses would go up a mountain or (later) into a place called "the tent of meeting," and he would meet with God face-to-face. He'd get all alone and have real one-on-one time with God. It was something of a secret rendezvous, an intimate conversation. Then Moses would go back to the Israelites and share what God had to say to them.

And check this out: we learn that whenever he left God's presence, Moses' face would be glowing.

Think about it. He had a *glowing* face. That's just weird. After a while that's got to bug your wife. "Would you turn that thing off, I'm trying to sleep!"

We're told that the people were afraid of glowing Moses.* And I can understand why. It's got to be freaky to have your friend glowing.

I get why they were afraid, but personally I'd enjoy having a friend with a luminous face. Moses would have been great for family fun . . . ("Hey Moses, it will be several thousand years until the power of electricity is harnessed and my kid can have an Easy-Bake oven, so until then could we just use your face?") Or on camping trips . . . ("We don't need a flashlight, just bring Moses!") Or if I was feeling lazy around Halloween and didn't want to carve a jack-o'-lantern . . . ("Hey Mo, would you hang out on my porch from 6:00 to 8:00? C'mon Moses, do it for the kids.")

So Moses would return from meeting with God with his face glowing. Then we learn that Moses would put a veil over his face, and he would only take the veil off when he went back to be with God. Then he'd come down, play the "Look at my glowy face" trick, and cover it up again.

Reading that, I have to wonder, "Why the veil?" I would guess that it was for everyone else's benefit. Perhaps Moses didn't want to bug people with his radiating head. And maybe he was worried they'd make fun of him:

"Do you also have a shiny heinie?"

"Knock, knock.—Who's there?—What do you mean who's there? Can't you see my face shining through the door? It's Moses!"

"How many Moseses does it take to screw in a light bulb?—None! He doesn't need a light bulb; his head is packing 200 watts all by itself!"

*That sounds like a great toy—"Glowing Moses." I bet I could make millions off of some homeschooled Christian kids if I marketed it. Wait a second.—Note to self: Mass produce Glowing Moses dolls! Possible marketing slogan: "Go for the Glo Mo!" Or, for more urban settings: "Go for Glo Mo, Fo Sho!"

But actually we're told why Moses veiled his face: "Moses . . . put a veil over his face to keep the Israelites from gazing at it *while the radiance was fading away.*"[1]

Why did Moses put the veil over his face? Because the radiance was fading away. It seems as though there must have been some embarrassment for Moses. He'd come back from God and people would be like, "Whoa! He's glowing! There are beams of light coming out of the brother's head!" But then Moses would wake up two days later and realize, "It's not as bright as it used to be." So he covered it up with a veil. Moses was no longer experiencing God as he had not so long ago, so he was now wearing the "I Climbed Mount Sinai and All I Got Was This Lousy Veil" so no one else would know that God's glory was fading from his life.

What we all want is to glow.

We go into this Christian thing, we read about it in the Bible, and we believe it's going to have a real impact on our lives. We should be able to *feel* it. It should *change* us. Other people should be able to see its effect. We want to glow.

But many of us, most of the time, are *not* glowing. And when we aren't glowing, like Moses, we cover our disappointment with a veil. We don't put on a literal veil; we use a veil of smiles and denials. Christians are famous (or *infamous*) for this. We wear fake, plastered smiles as a twisted badge of honor, pretending that everything's great all the time. We say things like, "It's another great day to praise the Lord!" "This is the day the Lord has made!" "What? No, nothing's wrong! God's blessings just keep getting better every day!" "God is good all the time!" We hide our true disappointment.

What should Moses have done? What should we do? Well, first, just be honest. Don't fake it. If you're not glowing, don't pretend you are.

But even better, when the glow starts to fade, get back in the tent of meeting!

The Christian life is about living life with Jesus. Living life with Jesus is about abiding in him. To abide means to *live within*. And so abiding is about living in the presence of: it's about depending on, it's about trusting in, it's about communicating with. To live life with Jesus, I *must* go into the tent of meeting and get *my* face in front of *his* face

It's like my marriage. My wife and I realized that with the busyness of life and all we had working against our relationship, we needed to start having a date night as the foundation upon which we built our date life. A date *life* was our goal, but a date *night* was a necessary part of establishing that.

What we're after with God is a *life* of abiding, a *continual* state of abiding. But to achieve that I need a concentrated period of abiding at some point in my day.

I know this sounds old school, but I'm convinced that the reason many of us are disappointed is because we don't spend nearly enough time in the "tent of meeting" face-to-face with God. And I think the two main components of that time are reading the Bible and praying. But we don't do that enough, and even when we do, we tend to approach it all wrong.

⁓

Often I'm guilty of approaching the Bible like it's a thing to check off my list—a religious obligation. But it's not.

Even more often I'm guilty of approaching the Bible like it's just something to teach me about God, and it's best delivered by others who are expert teachers. Now the Bible does teach me about God, and that is important, but that's *not* its primary purpose.

When my wife and I went to that counselor, his advice was not, "You two need to gather all the information you can about each other." Learning more information about each other wouldn't have hurt, but it wouldn't have helped much either. And if all the Bible does is give me information about God, it's not going to do much for my relationship with him.

Also, can you imagine if that counselor said, "Why don't you hire a professional presenter to give seminars to you each week providing lots of information about your spouse"? That would be ridiculous. But that's the way we sometimes approach God, as if we need experts to get to him. This is why so many Christians say this really strange thing: "I'm not getting *fed* at my church. My preacher's sermons are not feeding me." Christians who say this are disappointed T-shirt wearers, and their complaint reveals a belief that getting more information about God is the solution, and if it comes from experts, all the better.

They're wrong.

And when I approach the Bible that way, *I'm* wrong. Just like my wife, God is not someone for me to know *about*, he's someone for me to *know*. I can know *about* God by having someone else present me with information about him, but I *know* God by spending time with him, face-to-face. That's what causes me to glow.

So how should I approach the Bible?

Like it's an opportunity for me to have a sacred conversation with God every day. It's my chance to go into the tent of meeting, one-on-one, face-to-face with God, and to come out glowing.

That may sound a little mystical, but it's true. I really believe that God can speak to us through the Bible. The approach I need to take with the Bible is that God will speak to me through it, and we will have a sacred conversation. And when I do, God *does* speak to me.

It may sound weird to say that God can speak specifically to us through the Bible, but you know what's even weirder? A God that *can't* speak to us. In the Bible, idol worshippers and those who practice false religions are chastised for their beliefs. Why? Because they worship a "god" who can't speak.[2] So I'm thinking that God can and does speak, the problem is most of us just aren't listening. And that's what's weird—we have a God who wants to speak to us, but we don't ask him to.

So before I read the Bible I pause for a minute and I say something like, "God, I'm going to be really tempted to just steamroll through this so I can say I did it and check it off my religious to-do list, but please help me to resist that temptation. And God, I'm going to be really tempted to read this just to learn some facts about you, but please help me to avoid making this a trivial pursuit. God, I want to pursue *you*. And I want to hear from you. Please speak to me through this Book today."

And most of the time he does.

Now I don't hear voices, but it's amazing what happens. Like I'll be reading stories that seem so out-of-date and so out-of-touch with my life, and I'll ask, "God, what in the world does this have to do with me? What do you want to say to me through *this*?" And I'll get quiet for a second, and most of the time I will get it.

One time I was reading this bizarre story in the Old Testament about some guy who says that if God gives him success in a battle, he will sacrifice whatever comes out of his house to greet him when he returns home. The guy was probably hoping it'd be his dog, but unfortunately his *daughter* comes running out of the house. And so he has his daughter destroyed. And I thought, *Okaayyy, today's Bible time is going to be a waste, because there*

*can't be anything God wants to tell me from this story.
It's not like I'm going to have my daughter killed anytime
soon. This guy was an idiot, and that's about it.* And then
I paused, and it was like God said, "Dude, *you're* the
idiot." He was like, "How often do you speak before you
think, just like the guy in this story, and how many times
does it end up destroying another person's reputation
or feelings, like the other day when you made the guy
you work with feel stupid because he didn't agree with
your idea."

Another time I was reading about how the early Christians were having this controversy because some of them
were buying meat that had been sacrificed to idols. Others were offended because they said it was like partici-
pating in a false religion. But the Christians who were
eating it were like, "C'mon, it's the same as the meat
they serve at McDonald's. So chill out and pass the A.1.
sauce." And I thought, *Riiight. So God, I promise not to
buy meat sacrificed to idols. If the butcher ever puts up a
little sign: "Reduced Ground Chuck Due to Participation
in Idol Sacrifice," I will not buy it, even if it's cheaper.* And
God was like, "Think about it, Vince. Do you ever judge
Christians for doing something that I never said was
wrong, it's just that *you* think it's wrong?" And I said,
"No, God, I don't think so." And he started showing me
several ways I do this.

There was another time I read about this woman who
gets caught in the act of adultery, and Jesus totally lets
her off the hook. And I was thinking how she was pretty
messed up, and God said, "Vince, she's you." And I told
God that I had never been caught in the act of anything,
and he was like, "Are you kidding? Every time you sin I
catch you in the act." And I asked God why that woman
didn't have to get stoned for her crime, and why I didn't
have to suffer for all my sins, and he said, "Because
Jesus did."

Now, again, you don't have to call the mental ward or the poltergeist exterminator. I'm not hearing voices. But God *does* speak to me. Well, check that. God does speak to me *when I approach the Bible the right way*. God speaks to me when I approach the Bible not as something to check off my religious obligation list and not as something just to teach me about God but instead as part of a sacred conversation I get to have with him. Like it's my chance to go into the tent of meeting, one-on-one, face-to-face with God. When I approach it that way, I come out glowing. And when I *don't* read the Bible, or when I *don't* approach it that way, I *don't* glow.

Unfortunately, I have the same problems with prayer. As with the Bible, I can approach prayer like it's a religious to-do item I need to cross off my list every day.

It's not.

Or I can approach prayer the same way that I used to write my Christmas list for Santa Claus: excited to have someone to present all my requests to but a little skeptical of whether I'll get everything I'm asking for. And sure, God does want us to present our requests to him, and he will answer, but prayer is *much* more than that. And getting stuff from God is *not* the primary purpose of prayer.

So how should I approach prayer?

I love the way a guy named Augustine put it. He said, "True, whole prayer is nothing but love."[3] Prayer is love. It's an expression of intimacy. It's sharing my life with God. It's melting my heart into his.

Brennan Manning is one of my favorite authors, and he used to be a pastor-type down in New Orleans. He tells this story how one morning he got a phone call from a woman who asked, "Is this Brennan Manning?"

"Yes."

The voice on the other end said, "I understand you're a minister."

"Yes."

"Well, I was wondering if you could come speak to my father, he's on his deathbed."

Manning agreed to come right over. The daughter let Manning in and told him her father was in his bedroom. Manning walked into a stale-smelling bedroom and saw an old man, barely awake, his head supported by a pillow, his body covered in blankets. Manning noticed an empty chair beside the bed. He smiled, "I see you're expecting me."

The man tried to prop himself up, but was unable. "No," he said, seeming a bit confused. "Who are you?"

Manning laughed and explained that he was a minister invited over by the man's daughter.

"So you're a minister," the man said. "I have a question for you."

The man said he had always believed in God and Jesus but never knew how to pray. Once he asked a preacher, who gave him a book on prayer. The man explained that on the first page there were several words he didn't know. He gave up reading it on page three.

A few years later he was talking to a friend at work named Joe, and he discovered that Joe was a Christian. He told Joe that he didn't know how to pray. Joe said, "Really? Well, here's what you do. Take an empty chair. Put it next to you. Picture Jesus sitting in that chair, and talk to him. Tell him how you feel about him, talk to him about your life, share your needs with him. That's it."

The man looked at Brennan Manning nervously. "I've been doing that for years now," he said, almost apologetically. "Is that wrong?"

Manning smiled. "No, that's great. You just keep doing that." They talked some more, and then Manning prayed and left.

The next week that man's daughter called again. She said, "I just want to let you know that my father died yesterday. Thank you for visiting him. He really enjoyed talking to you."

Manning told her it was no problem and said, "I hope he died peacefully."

The daughter explained, "Well, it was interesting. I had to go to the store yesterday so I went in my dad's bedroom. He seemed fine. He made some corny joke, and I left. When I came back he was dead." She paused, then continued, "But here's the strange part, he had crawled out of his bed and he died with his head lying on that empty chair."[4]

Prayer is laying my head on God's lap.

Another author, Richard Foster, describes an event that likewise captures the essence of prayer. He writes:

One day a friend of mine was walking through a shopping mall with his two-year-old son. The child was in a particularly cantankerous mood, fussing and fuming. The frustrated father tried everything to quiet his son, but nothing seemed to help. The child simply would not obey. Then, under some special inspiration, the father scooped up his son and, holding him close to his chest, began singing an impromptu love song. None of the words rhymed. He sang off key. And yet, as best he could, this father began sharing his heart.

"I love you," he sang. "I'm so glad you're my boy. You make me happy. I like the way you laugh."

On they went from one store to the next. Quietly the father continued singing off key and making up words that did not rhyme. The child relaxed and became still, listening to this strange and wonderful song. Finally, they finished shopping and went to the car. As the father opened the door and prepared to buckle his son into the car seat, the child lifted his head and said simply, "Sing it to me again, Daddy! Sing it to me again!"[5]

Prayer is allowing myself to be gathered up into the arms of my heavenly Father, and listening as he sings his love songs over me.[6]

Another great picture of prayer comes from a time when Mother Teresa was interviewed on TV. She was asked, "What do you do when you pray?"

She answered, "I just listen."

The interviewer paused and then asked, "Well, what does God say?"

And Mother Teresa smiled and said, "I don't expect you to understand this, but he just listens."

I'm not sure *I* completely understand, but I think I know something of what she's getting at. I remember having girlfriends back when I was middle school age, and we would talk on the phone for hours, and we'd run out of things to say, but we didn't want to hang up. So we'd sigh and say, "Let's just listen to each other breathe."

Then after a few minutes I'd say, "Hey, are you still there?!"

And she'd say, "Yeah."

Then finally I'd be like, "Well, I have to go now."

"Yeah, me too."

"Okay," I'd say, "but you hang up first."

"No, you hang up first."

"Okay, but let's just wait a couple more minutes."

Couple of minutes later, "Are you still there?"

"Yeah."

Prayer is when you and God just listen to each other breathe.

We dream of a date life with God. We long for the kind of relationship with him where when people tell us we need to have a time where we focus on God each day, we laugh behind their backs.

Our entire lives are focused on God.

So much pulls our attention away from God, causes our intimacy with him to dwindle, and snuffs out our sense of adventure. So let me play counselor for you for a moment.

If you used to have a great relationship with God, you need to do the things you used to do. And if you never have, then you need to make whatever changes are necessary so you can start spending large quantities of quality time with God—face-to-face. It needs to be face-to-face.

When you do that, you'll come away glowing.

And what we all want is to glow.

MONK

9

In this chapter I'm taking on the monks. I wanted to have one sure victory in my book, and I feel confident they won't retaliate. I considered the Amish, the permanently comatose, or handicapped kids, but I settled on monks.

The unfortunate part of taking on the monks is that I will lose the endorsements I wanted from their community. Some quotes I was hoping for were:

"This book is monktastic!"

"We give it two thumbs monk, way monk!"

"Run, don't walk, from your monastery to the nearest bookstore to buy *T-Shirt*—reading it will monk you forever."

"*Lousy T-Shirt* is so good I wish I could eat it! It'd be monkalicious!"

I'm assuming here that monks like to use the word "monk" a lot. I'm pretty sure they're similar to the Smurfs in that way.

⌒

Living life with Jesus is about abiding in him. But what does it look like to abide? I believe it starts in the "tent of meeting"—as I have a focused time with God where I get my face before his face. But wouldn't it stink if that was *it*?

In helping my wife and me with our marriage, the counselor strongly encouraged that we start going on date nights, and that was wise advice, but what if that was *it*? What if our entire marriage consisted exclusively of a weekly date night? That wouldn't be much of a marriage.

If I enter into an abiding relationship with God, but it's just a short segment of my day, of course I'll be disappointed.

But that's *not* it.

Jesus' invitation was not simply to have a scheduled appointment with him each day but to live inside of him. He said, "Abide in Me" and "I am with you always."[1] The Bible explains what God is looking for: "Be joyful always; pray continually, give thanks in all circumstances, for this is God's will for you in Christ Jesus."[2] The words that pop out at me are "always," "continually," and "in all circumstances." Nowhere in the Bible do I get the idea that living life with Jesus is about a segment of my day.

However, I have found that segment of my day to be critical. It fixes my focus on God and sets me up to spend the rest of my day with him. But I need to remember, God is not looking for a date night with me, he's looking for a date *life*.

⌒

Early on in my Christian life someone gave me a book called *The Practice of the Presence of God* by a guy named Brother Lawrence, a monk. Reading a book by a monk sounded about as exciting as getting a root canal for twelve hours while sitting in front of a TV showing nonstop C-SPAN.

Still, I started reading, and this short book by this odd little man had to be the strangest book I ever read. But there was also something beautiful about it. Brother Lawrence decided he wanted to spend every moment of his life with God. That's actually the wrong way to say it, because God *is* with us always, and so we *do* spend every moment with him, whether we decide to or not. So it's more like Brother Lawrence decided he wanted to spend every moment of his life *aware* that God was with him. He called this "practicing God's presence." It's the act of focusing on the fact that God is present, of being careful not to ignore God.[3]

So I read this book and realized that Brother Lawrence was on to something. *This* was abiding. *This* was what living life with Jesus looked like. It was enjoying God's company, conversing lovingly with him in every moment. And this was the life that would overcome my disappointment and lead me to the romance and adventure with God that my heart longed for.

But I also realized that Brother Lawrence was a monk. And so I wondered, "Can *I* do it?" It's one thing to try to focus on God all day when you're a monk, perhaps with a vow of silence to keep you focused and the most exciting entertainment of the day is making bread. It's another when you're me living in a world of noise and action and children who want your attention along with the neighbor kid who keeps playing guitar in his garage.

I decided to read a little more about monks.

I learned that monks were driven by their need to escape from the world. One monk named Thomas Merton said, "Society . . . was regarded as a shipwreck from which each single individual man had to swim for his life."[4] These men (and sometimes women) would flee to the desert or to a monastery.

One aspect of a monk's flight is what was *left behind*—the evils of society, people who might lead to distraction, the temptations of this world. For instance, one of these guys was named Simeon the Stylite. Simeon fled society and entered a monastery. However, after ten years in a monastery, he decided that there were still too many distractions, still too much of the world, plus he believed God had told him he was no longer allowed to move. (Weird!) So Simeon built a little hut to live in, and chained himself to a pole in the middle in case he was tempted to leave. He ate as little as possible and tried to never sit or lie down. But a problem soon developed. People started showing up to ask Simeon to pray for them. Simeon could not tolerate the distractions of people requiring prayer, so he built a ten-foot-high pillar and took up residence on the top. Unfortunately, ten feet was not enough distance to fully eliminate distractions and all those pesky people, so Simeon kept building bigger pillars, finally perching himself atop one that was sixty feet high. And Simeon the Stylite spent *thirty-five years* living on that pillar.

The other aspect of a monk's flight is what was *being pursued*—the goal of a monk's life is what's called *hesychasm*. The term comes from the Greek word *hesychia*. In the New Testament, *hesychia* is translated "pray continually." Literally, the word *hesychia* means "come to rest." And so when the Bible tells us to "pray continually," there's the idea of coming to a place of rest in God, of resting in his presence.[5] And this is the goal of a monk's flight—to leave behind the evils of society, distractions of people, and temptations of this world in hopes of seeking solitude and silence as a means to rest in God's presence and pray continually to him. A

Russian monk named Theophan the Recluse explained their objective, "To pray is to descend with the mind into the heart, and there to stand before the face of the Lord."[6] Another monk, Macarius the Great, said, "The chief task of the athlete [that is, the monk] is to enter into [God's] heart."[7]

Okay, so after reading all this, here are some conclusions I came to.

First, something happens out there in the desert or within the confines of the monastery that causes monks' brains to become a little scrambled. Like who names himself "Theophan the Recluse" or "Macarius the Great"? If I named myself "Vince the Easily Agitated" or "Vince the Sexy Hunk of Beef," wouldn't someone surround me with padded walls? And what's the deal with Macarius the Great referring to monks as "athletes"? Have you ever seen an athletic monk? Macarius the Delusional is more like it.

Second, I'm glad I'm not a monk and don't have to live in a monastery. I've actually given this some thought, and would like to share with you . . .

The Top Ten Reasons I'm Glad I Don't Live in a Monastery

10. Brown is not my color.
 9. Hard to do the Macarena to a Gregorian chant.
 8. It would be tough explaining my wife and kids to the "Monk Superior."
 7. *Baywatch* poster down. Mother Teresa poster up!
 6. Fear that I might be "it" in the weekly game of "Dunk the Monk."
 5. I don't think the haircut would look good on me.
 4. Wool robes tend to chafe.
 3. Hard to impress local girls with pickup line, "Hey baby, I've taken a vow of poverty."
 2. One word: Celibacy.
 1. They won't accept my idea: Monk by day, ninja by night.

Third, I think monks have an image problem. In fact, I want to go see some monk representatives and share some marketing slogans I've been dreaming up. Here's a few:

"If Silence Is Golden, We've Hit the Jackpot!"
"What Happens in the Monastery, Stays in the Monastery"
"We Don't Wear Anything under These Robes!"
"Bland Food: It's Not Just for the English Anymore"
"Putting the 'Monk' in 'Monkey Business'"

Fourth, I think monks have it *half* right. I have questions about whether Jesus would want any of his followers to escape from the world. I think their doing so is well-intentioned but misguided.[8] But I *love* their goal. Their desire to practice the presence of God, to find joy in his company, to talk with him moment-by-moment—I think that's what *we're* missing.

So I was excited about what the monks were attempting but discouraged by what they felt they had to do to achieve it. I wasn't about to leave my wife and kids, to take a vow of silence, or to live on a pole. So was living life with Jesus, abiding, and hesychasm not an option for me? Because what I wanted was half different than the monks:

The monks flee from distractions so they can pray without ceasing. I wanted to pray without ceasing in the midst of distractions.

The monks live in isolation so they won't be pulled away from God by others. I wanted to live in community with others so they can help pull me towards God.

The monks build a monastery so they can stay there and stay focused on God. I want to *be* a monastery so I can always stay focused on God no matter where I go.

I struggled with all this for a while, but then I came across examples of people who shared the same goal as the monks but didn't feel it necessary to escape society. One was a guy named Frank Laubach. Laubach was a teacher and a missionary to Muslim tribes in the Philippines. At the age of forty-five he felt like he had wasted his time and, basically, his life. But then he had a defining moment at a place called Signal Hill. In the next forty years, Laubach became one of the most widely known and loved men in the world. He wrote over fifty-five books, several of which became bestsellers with worldwide influence. He is considered by many to be the best educator of modern times. The organization he started helped over 100 million people learn how to read. He even got his face on a U.S. postage stamp. So what happened at Signal Hill?

At Signal Hill, Frank Laubach made a decision to spend the rest of his life focusing on God. He devoted himself to looking for God and listening to God throughout each moment of every day. He dedicated himself to being attentive to the opportunities God might be presenting him and to seize each of those opportunities. This became his lifelong goal, as he wrote in his journal: "Can I bring the Lord back in my mind flow every few seconds so that God shall always be in my mind? I choose to make the rest of my life an experiment in answering this question." I bet that Frank Laubach didn't achieve his goal of focusing on God *all* the time *perfectly*, but I also bet he rarely was ever disappointed or bored after making that decision. And the decision he made at the age of forty-five to spend the rest of his days living life with Jesus, abiding in him, being a flightless monk who practiced hesychasm, changed his life, and the world.

Another person I read about was Etty Hillesum. Etty Hillesum was a young girl who became a prisoner at the Auschwitz concentration camp during World War II. She kept a journal during her stay at Auschwitz and in it she recorded her goal of an "uninterrupted dialogue" with God. Author Philip Yancey writes about her:

> She had epiphanies even in that most barren place. "Sometimes when I stand in some corner of the camp, my feet planted on Your earth, my eyes raised toward Your Heaven, tears sometimes run down my face, tears of deep emotion and gratitude." She knew the horror. "And I want to be there right in the thick of what people call horror and still be able to say: life is beautiful." Hillesum concluded, "For once you have begun to walk with God, you need only keep on walking with God and all of life becomes one long stroll—a marvelous feeling."[9]

Yancey concludes, "I . . . wonder what I might have written in my private journal as I breathed in ashes from the ovens each day . . . Yes, walking with God makes life one long stroll—but for how many, and how often, is it a marvelous feeling?"[10] So what was it that allowed Etty Hillesum to overcome the horror of her surroundings? Why didn't she succumb to despair? It's because her goal was an "uninterrupted dialogue" with God. Living life with Jesus, abiding, and hesychasm is what leads us to life fully alive.

And Laubach and Hillesum didn't flee from the world. They stayed focused on God in the midst of everyday life. And that made me think I could too.

Little by little I'm understanding what this looks like. The monks have a theological idea they call *perichoresis*. They believe that God the Father, Jesus, and the Holy Spirit exist together in a sort of choreographed dance of love.[11] Since the beginning of time they've been tangoing, moving together in a beautiful embrace. And we are invited into that dance.[12] We get to spend our days *dancing* with God. In fact, we were created in God's image, and so if God is always dancing, *we* were designed to dance too. Our lives were meant to be a dance with God—and a dance is passionate, interactive, fun at times, romantic at others.

Abiding looks like a dance with God. Now when you dance with someone it's typically awkward at first. You're very aware of what you're doing, of what the other person is doing, of the correct steps you're supposed to be taking. But when people continue dancing together, eventually it becomes totally comfortable. You stop having to think about what you or the other person is doing or the correct steps to follow. It all becomes very natural. In fact, if you watch people who can *really* dance, it's sometimes almost hard to tell where one person ends and the other begins.

And that's what God is after with us. That's what abiding looks like. It's a moment-by-moment sharing of life with him that may be awkward at first. In the beginning it may take great conscious effort. And there may be embarrassing trips and falls and stepping on toes. But slowly it becomes more and more instinctive, effortless, and enjoyable. Eventually, we might even come to a place where it's not that I have to practice the presence of God and remember to focus on and spend my time with him. It will be like we're one person, connected and "lost" in each other.

Earlier I mentioned that I went on a fifteen-day trip to Vietnam. It was the longest I had ever been away from my wife. A day after I returned home I had to go back to work. My kids were at school, so I asked my wife if she would come and hang out in my office during the day. She said, "What am I supposed to do? Don't you have work you have to get done?" I told her I did, but I wanted to be around her and she could bring things to do of her own. And so Jen brought a backpack full of bills to pay and magazines to read and sat at the table in my office while I sat at my desk.

Throughout the day I occasionally had conversations with her (I'd say, "Hey, tell me about how that party I missed went . . ." or she'd begin, "On your trip, did you ever get to . . ."), and we'd talk for several minutes. Once in a while I would comment on what I was doing ("Oh, I can't believe this email. Listen to this . . .") or she'd remark about something to me ("This article is really interesting. Did you know . . ."). Often I'd look over and smile at her or catch a glimpse of her smiling at me. Much of the time I wasn't really talking to her or looking at her, but I *always* knew she was there. Well, perhaps there were a few moments when I forgot, but then quickly I'd remember, "Oh yeah, Jen's with me today."

I think that's what it looks like to abide throughout my day with God. My day of abiding starts by going into the tent of meeting, but then I leave, and rather than fleeing from the world, I dive into it. I've got all kinds of things to do, all kinds of people with whom I have to interact, plus I've got traffic to get through and some TV to watch—but my goal is to do all of that *with* God.

There may be a few spots where I actually have conversations with him (I'll say, "Hey God, I've got some time while I wait here. I wanted to talk to you about these feelings of resentment I've been having towards . . ." or he'll initiate it by, say, filling me with this deep sense of gratitude over something I normally take for granted), and we'll talk for a couple of minutes. And often I'll just kind of smile, knowing that I'm not going through my day alone (and that he's smiling at me).

Most of the day I won't exactly be talking to God or even looking in his direction, but I know he's there. Well, the truth is that it's really easy for me to forget God is there and to ignore him for a while, and that's why I need to discipline myself and remember, "Oh yeah, God is with me today."

So how do we discipline ourselves to practice the presence of God, to maintain that inner dialogue with him, especially in the first stages when it's still new and awkward to us? Here are a few ideas I've picked up.

First, again, is to start my day by centering myself with God by going into the tent of meeting and getting my face in front of his. I've found that if I don't start my day that way, I have very little chance of spending the rest of my day focused on God.

Second, I need reminders the rest of my day. Back in Jesus' day there were no clocks, but there were bells from the Roman forum that would ring out at 6:00 a.m., 9:00 a.m., noon, 3:00 p.m., and 6:00 p.m. Jewish people of the day used this as their schedule for daily prayers, and the early Christians continued this practice.[13] Most of us don't hear bells chiming throughout the day, and therefore many find it helpful to create their own reminders. I know people who set their watch to ding every hour on the hour, and each time they hear it ask themselves, "Am I practicing God's presence right now? Am I aware that he's with me? Are we in a dialogue?" If not, they use that to call their attention back to God. I know others who wear a bracelet so every time they see it they're reminded to pray. Another idea is to set specific prayer times throughout the day. I have a friend who uses his drive to work to visually pray through what kind of person he wants to be at work that day, asking God for the strength to do it. Then on his drive home he visually prays through playing with his son, spending time with his wife, again asking God to help him be the man he's meant to be.

Third, I need to look for flickers of God in unexpected places. The ancient Celtics believed in what they called "thin places." These are places where the natural and supernatural worlds come together at their narrowest, with only a thin veil between them. When you're in a thin place you're able to catch a glimpse of God, and it becomes easier to sense his presence.

Have you ever watched a movie and suddenly had your heart clench up? Something happened in the movie and for a moment you came alive. Maybe it was from the romance or it was a hero overcoming the odds and accomplishing victory. Something almost otherworldly grabbed you. What happened, and why? Perhaps it was that the story you saw portrayed on the screen was really God's story. In that romance your soul's longing to be loved by God was awoken. In the victory your soul celebrated Jesus' triumph over death and yearned for the day when you will join him. That theater had become a thin place. God was reminding you of his presence.

Maybe you've had a similar experience driving down the road. Radio blaring, singing along, then stop—a phrase in the song sparked for you; it was something in the words. It sent you soaring. Your car had become a thin place.

Or you were walking along on the beach and you looked up at a mesmerizing sunset. You couldn't take your eyes off it. Without thinking you found yourself saying thank you. To what? To whom? You hadn't even thought about God in who knows how long, but something inside breaks open and is filled with a divine warmth. That beach had become a thin place.

You could barely see the road through the snow but you had no choice except to drive in it. All of a sudden your car was spinning. A concrete median on one side, a truck on the other. You found yourself crying out, "God, help me!" The weird thing is that you didn't believe in God at the time. That icy road had become a thin place.

A few months ago I was at a water park, floating around a "lazy river" with my kids. They had each taken on new nicknames: "Tamale" and "Coconut." We were laughing hysterically, having the time of our life. It was inexpressible joy. The thought occurred to me, *I hope heaven is like this.* That water park had become a thin place.

God knows it's difficult for us to remember that he's with us, so he does all kinds of things to capture our attention. We need to pay attention and look for those flickers of God in unexpected places.

Fourth, it helps me to lay down a beat. If the goal is abiding (and as I've learned from the monks, abiding is a lot like dancing), it helps to have music. Dancing without music is far more difficult than with music. And so at times I've found it helpful to lay down a beat. I read about this anonymous Russian monk from the nineteenth century who set out to live in unceasing communion with God. He wrote a book called *The Way of the Pilgrim.* In this book he explains how he made it his practice to repeatedly say a prayer in his mind, "Lord Jesus Christ, Son of God, have mercy on me, a sinner."[14] Eventually, that prayer became so internalized he found himself praying it without even trying. Contemporary author Anne Lamont seeks to repeatedly say one of her two favorite prayers, "Thank you, thank you, thank you," or "Help me, help me, help me."[15] Choosing a consistent prayer can help lay a beat and provide music for our dance with God.

⁓

Monks have taught me that I've been invited into the dance of God. It doesn't come naturally to dance with God, and so I understand why monks flee off to be by themselves. I mean it's easier to dance with a partner on some secluded island. But I believe we've been called to tango with God on a crowded dance floor. That can be a very self-conscious place. And there are a lot of distractions out on the dance floor, including people to bump into. Perhaps it'd be easier not to dance at all. And that is what many choose. But many are disappointed, and I choose not to be disappointed. I choose to dance, to dance the dance of the flightless monk.

PART 3

PROGRESS

NEW LIFE, NEW SHIRT

ABOUND

10

If you invited me to your church this Sunday to speak, here's how I think I'd start my message: "Stop trying to be like Jesus." I probably wouldn't be invited back, and people might think I'm joking, but I'm serious. I think one of our biggest problems is that we're trying to be like Jesus.

He's not the first person I've tried to be like.

The year was 1984. I was fourteen years old and finally realized what I wanted to be in life. I wanted to be a basketball player. More specifically, I wanted to be just like Michael Jordan. I went out and bought Air Jordans. Just like Mike wore. I got some Nike shorts and shirts because that's what Mike wore. Whenever I soared through the sky for my dunks, I would stick my tongue out and kick my feet to the side, just like Mike did. (In the interest of integrity, and to make sure I don't end up being scolded by Oprah on her TV show, I must admit that the only place I dunked was in my bedroom, with my Nerf ball, on my six-foot-high hoop.) Seriously though, I practiced basketball hard. I devoted myself to having a Jordan-like game. I went out first thing in the morning and was often still on the court after dark. I guzzled Gatorade and wore Hanes underwear. But as committed as I was, I never even came close to approaching Jordan-esqueness. My game improved a little, but it was obvious I could never be a great basketball player.

I'll never forget the day I sat on the living room couch, crying my eyes out, "Why? Why can't I become an NBA player? Why can't I be like Mike?"

"I don't know, dear," my four-foot-eleven mother replied, "but at least you gave it your all."

By 1987 I left behind my Michael Jordan aspirations for a new dream. I wanted to be a singer. More specifically, I wanted to be just like Axl Rose, frontman for the then wildly popular, American hard rock band Guns N' Roses. I dyed my hair red and grew it long, wearing a bandana around it. I wouldn't wear a shirt, except the one tied around my waist. I practiced swiveling my hips to "Welcome to the Jungle" for hours in front of a full-length mirror. I tried to fully transform into Axl Rose. This led to a drug addiction, a few car accidents, and my starting a riot at a Metallica concert. I also began calling guys "Slash" and the ladies, "Sweet Child o' Mine." You could hear me mumbling about living in the jungle and how I couldn't wait to move to Paradise City, and that my ultimate goal was writing the perfect album. And I sang. I sang and sang and sang. I "Do-Re-Mi-ed" and worked on my vocal range and tried to harmonize with anything I could—the radio, my sister, the microwave, cats in heat. But no matter what I did, I never sounded anything like Axl Rose or, for that matter, any professional singer. One night I finally lost it, broke down, and sobbed, "Why? Why can't I become a professional singer? Why can't I be like Axl?"

"I don't know, dear," said my tone-deaf mother, "but at least you gave it your all."

More recently I've tried really hard to be like Jesus. In 1990 I became a Christian, and even my first cursory reading of the New Testament led me to understand that being like Jesus was God's goal for my life. Like the Bible says, "From the beginning God decided that those who came to him . . . should become like his son . . ."[1] And it wasn't just that God wanted me to be like Jesus, *I* wanted to be like Jesus. I had been examining his life and had come to the inescapable conclusion that he was the coolest person and had led the most extraordinary life that I had ever come across.

So I went for it. I didn't buy a WWJD bracelet, but I might as well have. I gritted my teeth, grunted a lot, swore I would stop committing some sins, and dedicated myself to being more disciplined.

Mostly, I failed.

I would occasionally improve, but not significantly. And often after taking a few steps forward I would take several back. No matter how hard I tried, I just couldn't pull it off.

I can remember *many* times lying in my bed, in the dark, near tears, crying out to God, "Why? Why can't I do this? Why can't I be like Jesus?"

But he didn't answer. I didn't hear anything. No matter how many times I asked . . . nothing.

Finally, I felt led to go back to the Bible and give it more than a cursory reading. Maybe I was wrong. Maybe God didn't expect me to become like Jesus? Maybe it was okay for me to continue unchanged?

Unfortunately, as I read the Bible again, slower and more carefully, I realized I *wasn't* wrong. God *did* want me to become like Jesus, and I *couldn't* just continue on without being transformed. In fact, I ran into some verses that made me feel worse. Like Jesus said, "I tell you the truth, anyone who has faith in me will do what I have been doing. He will do *even greater things* than these, because I am going to the Father."[2] So I was not only supposed to be like Jesus but actually do *greater* things than him?

And the Bible said, "Be steadfast, immovable, always *abounding* in the work of the Lord."[3] I looked up the word *abound*—hoping that perhaps it had been translated poorly into English. It's translated from the Greek word *perisseuō*, which means to superabound, be in excess, be superfluous, or to excel.[4] Unbelievable! So not only do I need to be like Jesus, and do greater things than him, but I have to *superabound* in it?

Now I wasn't only disappointed, I was depressed. The Bible said I should abound. And though I had been trying my hardest, my results were closer to abysmal than abounding.

Why wasn't I abounding?

I continued to read and ultimately I came to the conclusion that Jesus wasn't talking about me striving to be like him. That's what I had been doing. I had been trying my hardest, but even with my best efforts it became obvious that really being like Jesus is impossible.

I realized that back as a fourteen-year-old I could have done a great imitation of a bad basketball player, but I could only do a bad imitation of a great basketball player. I just didn't have it in me to become a great basketball player.

And I realized that as a seventeen-year-old I could have done a great imitation of a bad singer, but I could only do a bad imitation of a great singer. I just didn't have it in me to become a great singer.

And as a twenty-year-old, I could have done a great imitation of someone with bad character living a bad life, but I could only do a bad imitation of someone with *great* character living a *great* life. That's why I couldn't be like Jesus. I just didn't have that in me.

Looking back, it's obvious that me trying to play like Jordan or sing like Axl were losing propositions, and I was bound for failure. And so I wondered if in wanting me to become like Jesus, God had given me a losing proposition and had set me up for failure. I didn't think so, but it seemed like it.

Then I came across another verse: "[God's] divine power has given us everything we need for life and godliness."[5] I noticed it didn't say that I *had* everything for life and godliness but that God had *given* me everything I needed for life and godliness. So to become like Jesus, God had to give me something. I read the next verse to find out what it was, where it continues: "[God] has given us his very great and precious promises, so that through them you may participate in *the divine nature* and escape the corruption in the world caused by evil desires."[6] What God had given me, to help me to become like Jesus, was the very nature of Jesus.[7] Finally, things began making sense to me. The reason I couldn't be like Jesus was because I just didn't have it in me, *but* if I had Jesus in me, that would be a whole different story.

And that made me think about the whole idea of abiding. So I went back and read again what Jesus said about abiding: "Abide in Me, and I in you. As *the branch cannot bear fruit of itself* unless it abides in the vine, so *neither can you, unless you abide in Me*. I am the vine, you are the branches; he who abides in Me and I in him, *he bears much fruit*; for *apart from Me you can do nothing*."[8]

Finally, it hit me: *abiding is the key to abounding*. I *can't* live the Jesus life, only Jesus can. And he wants to live his life *through* me. The key isn't me striving to be like Jesus but instead me *abiding* in Jesus.

It's like that humidifier in my bedroom. I can't be the presence of Jesus in other peoples' lives if I'm not filled with Jesus myself.

And I started trying to do that, and I've been finding that it really works. As I live life with Jesus—by going into the tent of meeting so I can have face time with him and then spending the rest of my day with a monklike focus on God—he will live his life through me. Finally, I've started living the Jesus life, but in a mysterious but very real sense it's not me who's living it.

When I'm abiding, I'm abounding.

And when I'm not abiding, I'm not abounding.

This has been *the* major breakthrough for me.

But I've learned that even if I do abide, there are still a few things that can hold me back from abounding. Maybe certain things hold you back too. So let me tell you what holds me back from abounding before we focus on what abounding in the Jesus life really looks like.

SPEED

11

In sections of Montana the speed limit used to be defined by words, not numbers. Drivers designated their own speed limit by what they deemed to be "reasonable and prudent." That was the speed limit. You were supposed to drive at a rate that was reasonable and prudent.

They clocked one guy going 150 miles per hour.

I laughed when I heard that, but then I realized . . . it's me. I get to set the speed limit for my life. No one else sets my speed limit. I do, and I'm rushing through everything I do. I'm going at 150 miles per hour.

I'm called to live life with Jesus, and to live the Jesus life, and only through that will I gain real life. But because of my speed, I often remain disappointed, and I find myself *losing* life.

In 1983 a movie came out called *Koyaanisqatsi*. Directed by Godfrey Reggio, it drew some interest because Academy Award–winning film director Francis Ford Coppola got behind it. The film opens with the soundtrack chanting, "Koyaanisqatsi, koyaanisqatsi, koyaanisqatisi, koyaanisqatsi, koyaanisqatsi, koyaanisqatisi"—and *then* it gets really weird. The movie has no plot, no narrative, and no dialogue. It's merely an eighty-seven-minute progression of photographed scenes, often moving at a frenetic pace.

This is the problem with living at 150 miles per hour. Life becomes a blur of images. I see it all go by, but I lose the plotline, the narrative, even the dialogue.

Really, I lose life.

I'm just skimming along the surface of life because I'm moving too fast and am just too busy to pause and invest time in my priorities.

And that's a real problem—because my priorities are what allow me to live the Jesus life, and that's the only way I can live life fully alive.

⌣

Someone once asked Jesus to pinpoint the most important commandment. Basically, this guy was asking Jesus to help him set his top priority. Jesus said, "Okay, here it is: Love God." But here's how Jesus put it to the guy: "I'll give you two commandments. The first priority is to love God; the second is to love people."[1] Then he added, "Do this and you will live."[2]

I love that part: "Do this and you will live."

Now I'm quite sure that the people listening to Jesus *were alive* when he spoke those words. He wasn't addressing dead people. He looked out at a bunch of *living* people and said, "If you want to live you have to really love God and love people."

Jesus seems to be saying that it's possible to live without really living. I think Jesus was speaking to every one of us. I think he was implying, "Some people are out enjoying the journey, the adventure, but many of you are missing it, and you're disappointed." Why? Because they weren't living the Jesus life. And, at its core, the Jesus life is about loving God and loving people.

It's impossible to love God or people in a hurry.

It's like I'm living too fast to really live.

Jesus not only taught about these top two priorities, he modeled them. Jesus had more life than any person I've encountered, and it came through deeply loving God and people. And Jesus could do that because he never hurried. There is never any indication that he was in a rush.

And that shouldn't surprise me, because Jesus was God. And God doesn't speed.

Perhaps the coolest named theologian, Kosuke Koyama, wrote,

God walks "slowly" because he is love. If he is not love he would have gone much faster. Love has its speed. It is an inner speed. It is a spiritual speed. It is a different kind of speed from the technological speed to which we are accustomed . . . It goes on in the depth of our life, whether we notice or not, whether we are currently hit by storm or not, at three miles an hour. It is the speed we walk and therefore it is the speed the love of God walks.[3]

This is what's holding me back from living the Jesus life. I'm going 150, but God moves at 3 miles per hour. So I need to slow down and walk at God's speed.

I need to move at the speed of love.

Seriously, I may be one of the best examples of 150-mph living on the planet. I get up early and rush through my time with God, fly over to work, try to get as much done at the office as I possibly can (often leaving people who need my attention in my dust), race home, shove food down my throat, hurry over to coach my son's baseball practice, sprint back to the car in hopes of getting to small group on time, try to accelerate the pace of the small group discussion because I have things to do at home, zip out the door at the amen of the closing prayer, race home (again), throw my kids in bed, get out my computer, tear through a few emails and try to complete a project I've been working on, realize how late it is, dash upstairs to bed, get insufficient sleep, and get up the next morning to do it all again.

I wish what I just wrote were hyperbole, but it's not. It's a reasonably accurate description of the normal rhythms of my life.

I just realized—I'm even trying to hurry through this chapter so this book will get finished. Wow! I am racing through a chapter on slowing down . . . in a book on living the Jesus life so I can get back to all the things I have to do in my normal life in which I'm constantly disappointed because I'm not living the Jesus life. Talk about crazy!

And the insanity of my pace is only highlighted by living with my wife, Jen. Getting married to Jen was like joining together a squirrel on amphetamines and a turtle on Valium. I move at the speed of light. Jen moves at the speed of love.

It's not like she doesn't have lots to do—she does, probably as much as I do. But somehow she manages to do it all at the speed of love.

For the past three years she's been going every week with our daughter to a nursing home. Every week Jen drives thirty minutes each way to this small, privately owned home where ten women and a parrot named Barney live. Every week some of the women introduce themselves to Jen again, like she hasn't already met them 140 times. Every week the women make the same jokes, tell the same stories, ask the same questions. Every week Jen laughs again at the same jokes, listens again to the same stories, answers again the same questions. Every week they sit together and watch a full mind-numbing hour of the estrogen-overflowing talk show *The View*. Every week the women get to watch my daughter as she shows them what it's like to be five again. And every week my daughter gets to watch my wife as she shows her what it's like to really love people. Very rarely does Jen get to share with them Jesus' message, but every week she shares with them his presence simply by showing up, by living her life at the speed of love.

Another thing Jen does every week is take our daughter to swim lessons. On occasion, I too have been the one to take our daughter to swim lessons. When I fill in, I always bring work to do, because it seems smart to cross things off my to-do list during that time. When Jen goes she never brings anything to do, because there will be other mothers, and they're more important than her to-do list.

One of the moms in the viewing area at swim lessons is Stephanie. Jen got to know Stephanie as they watched their kids flounder around in the pool. After a few weeks Stephanie shared with Jen that her other child who was only three years old, had died eleven months earlier of a genetic disorder. Jen cried with her, asked questions, and listened. At the end of the hour Stephanie thanked Jen, explaining that she hadn't really felt comfortable sharing that with many people; and the few she had told never seemed to care. "They probably care," Jen responded, "maybe they just don't know what to say." Stephanie agreed and thanked Jen for *showing* her compassion, not just feeling it.

Last week was the anniversary of the death of Stephanie's child. Jen bought her a gift to help Stephanie celebrate the years she was able to share with her daughter and wrote her an encouraging card. She sat forever at the kitchen table writing it, picking out each word carefully, doing the whole thing at the speed of love.

Speaking of losing a child, a few years ago we were up in Buffalo at Jen's parents' home. The day after Christmas we received a phone call from my sister. She was six months pregnant with her first child. She and her husband, Jay, had already chosen a name—Julia. But my sister just found out she had lost the baby a day earlier, on Christmas Day. She was going to have to deliver the fetus the next morning. We told her we'd drive down immediately. We packed up, got in the car, and started on the twelve-hour drive to North Carolina. My sister is a Christian, but her husband is not. Neither is my mother, who was already there with them in the hospital. I had spent years praying for them, trying to look for openings to talk to them about God's love for them and their need for Jesus. As we drove I realized that although I didn't want to be opportunistic at such a difficult time, this might be a special chance to talk to them. I think Jen felt the same way.

I called my sister at the hospital from my cell phone, telling her we'd arrive around nine or ten at night. She asked if when we arrived, I could read her something appropriate from the Bible. She said her husband and our mother would be there as well. I hung up, and then as I drove I thought through what I would do when we arrived. After a few hours, I had my plan.

We arrived at the hospital, hugged, and talked. Finally, my sister asked if I would read her something encouraging from the Bible. I got out my Bible and read a story from the Old Testament when King David's baby dies and he says, "I will go to him, but he will not return to me." I explained that David had confidence that he would see his child in heaven. Then I read a story from the New Testament, where Jesus' friend Lazarus dies and everyone mourns. But Jesus raises him from the dead and all the people rejoice at his resurrection. I told my sister "You know, this doesn't mean we're not sad now. Honestly, it hardly makes me feel better at all, but still I *know* that you and I are going to spend all of eternity with Julia in heaven."

And then I looked at my mother with tears in my eyes and said, "But I don't think you will." I turned to my brother-in-law and said, "And I don't think you will either." I told them, "That *totally* breaks my heart. Listen, I'm sure I'm going to be in heaven, because I've studied Jesus' life and the evidence for it, and I know that his death has the power to take my sins away because I've put my faith in him. If someone studied it and somehow came to the conclusion that it wasn't true and rejected it, well, okay, at least they made an informed choice. But I can't understand how you guys know people who *have* studied it and are positive it's true, and you won't even take the time to check it out. And my prayer is that your knowing that there may possibly be a heaven, and that Julia will be there, will be the thing that leads you to study about Jesus, and to decide if it's true or not, and I pray you put your faith in him. And, like I said, that hardly makes what's happening right now any better— it's still horrible, but it would be better to spend all of eternity together than just a few years here on earth."

They listened politely. They didn't get angry. They thanked me, but my words have had no impact on their lives.

I had tried to love them, but I realize now that I did it at 150 miles per hour. I flew into the room, tried to encapsulate everything I wanted to say into a brief "presentation" and hoped to see immediate results.

Jen handled the whole situation differently. She prayed on the drive, as I did. She walked into the hospital room, as I did. She hugged everyone and sat and talked, as I did. But as I read the stories and challenged my mother and brother-in-law, she just sat there. And a few minutes later when I left to take my kids to my sister's home to go to sleep, Jen stayed and spent the night sleeping in a chair in the hospital room. The next morning when my sister had to deliver the fetus, Jen was standing next to her, holding her hand. I left North Carolina to return home and go back to work two days later. Jen stayed for another week.

Jen didn't see any immediate results, and hasn't seen any significant results since then either (though, unlike me, I'm not sure she was really looking for any particular results). But now, when my sister needs someone to talk to or some advice, or wants someone praying for her, guess who she calls? Jen. Why? Because my sister needs someone who moves at the speed of love. And if you asked my mother or brother-in-law if I offended them with my speech in the hospital room, I'm quite sure they'd say no, that I did it in a very sensitive way and they know it came from a caring heart. But if you asked them who really impressed them in that whole crisis, or who'd they turn to if they needed someone, I'm sure they'd both answer—Jen. Why? Because she moves at the speed of love.

If I'm going to get serious about living the Jesus life, I need to slow down. But sometimes that seems impossible, because my life just keeps getting crazier and crazier.

And I've tried to make some self-initiated attempts to slow myself down, but any success they bring is brief at best. So I've started turning to God and asking him how I'm supposed to slow down.

His answer is . . . Sabbath.

God has a plan for slowing me down and it's called Sabbath. The idea is that, with his help, I will discipline myself to slow down on one day each week, and then it will start to spread to the rest of my life.

Sabbath is a commandment of God given in the Old Testament,[4] but it's not meant to bind us. Rather, it's meant to give us the freedom to really live. It's meant to slow us down so we can really love God and love people, which can only happen at 3 miles per hour.

I'd had a little success at practicing the discipline of Sabbath and even of seeing it slowly spread to reduce the speed at which I live the other days of my life. But it still wasn't quite doing the trick. And so finally, I had to flip the script on the way I thought about Sabbath.

I used to think I had to live out the Sabbath so I could live life with Jesus, but now I believe I have to live life with Jesus so I can live out the Sabbath.

When I first encountered the idea of Sabbath, I thought of it as just a command to follow. So it was sort of like a jail cell . . . it felt very confining, like I was bound up in rules and boundaries. But then I moved to a slightly more correct and somewhat healthier view of Sabbath, thinking of it as a day off or a brief chance to escape life's demands. But I've moved on from that as well. Now I think of Sabbath as a *person*.

I've come to believe that Jesus was not only God in the flesh; he also incarnated Sabbath.

As I mentioned, Jesus never hurried and was never in a rush. He had thousands of people who wanted his time, who wanted his attention, who wanted his touch, who wanted to experience his teaching and miracles. But still Jesus managed to do life in such a way that he never had to hurry. He never said, "Oh shoot! Let's bust our butts and get over to Capernaum, quick! People need me!" We never see him run.

In fact, Jesus was given thirty-three years on earth to start a world-changing revolution, and he waited thirty years to begin. Finally, he came out of obscurity and was baptized, now ready to launch his ministry, and what did he do first? He went into the desert, back into isolation, and spent forty days alone with God, fasting and praying in solitude.

When he finally embarked on his ministry, he repeatedly took time to rest, to spend with his closest friends, to get away by himself, to pray.

Jesus' method of caring for people was to focus on the person standing right in front of him. I typically view the person in front of me as an obstacle to accomplishing my true mission, but Jesus viewed the person in front of him *as* his true mission.

Jesus knew how to say no. He would leave the crowds behind to go off and commune with his Father. And I'm sure people would question him, "Jesus, all of these people are hungry. Many need healing. You are their only hope. And you're going to leave them? You're going to go *pray?*" But that's exactly what he did. He left them. He prayed.

Jesus said, "Are you tired? Worn out? Burned out on religion? Come to me. Get away with me and you'll recover your life. I'll show you how to take a real rest. Walk with me and work with me—watch how I do it. Learn the unforced rhythms of grace. I won't lay anything heavy or ill-fitting on you. Keep company with me and you'll learn to live freely and lightly."[5]

⌒

Jesus offers to help me because I am rhythmically challenged. By walking with him I learn to slow down and live at the speed of love.

When I do life at 150 miles per hour, I lose life. I have a hurried life of not really loving God or people. I have a life of missed moments. I have a life without plotline, narrative, or dialogue. I have koyaanisqatsi.

Koyaanisqatsi is a Hopi Indian word. It means "life out of balance," or "crazy life," or "life in turmoil." The Hopi Indians used it to describe someone whose life is in such a disintegrating state that it calls for that person to find another way of living. Life at 150 miles per hour is koyaanisqatsi.

How do I recover life? By doing life with Jesus at 3 miles per hour. If I were to walk with God at the spiritual speed

of love it will lead me to an intentional life of deeply loving God and people, a life of being fully present in every
moment, a life of Sabbath rest. There's a Hebrew word in
the Old Testament related to Sabbath that expresses what
happens when we live this way. It is the word *vyinafesh*
in Exodus 23:12, which means to "rest, be refreshed, i.e.,
to cease from an activity, resulting in rest and refresh-
ment from a weary state."[6] So vyinafeshing connotes a
refreshing that continually builds up the soul.

This is our choice: koyaanisqatsi or vyinafeshing. Will
we speed through life at 150 miles per hour with a disintegrating soul? Or we will walk with Jesus at 3 miles
an hour with a soul that is continually restored?

If we want to keep pace with God, we *must* change
our speed.

Koyaanisqatsi or vyinafeshing?

NAKED

12

When my kids were a little younger they had this strange ritual at bath time. They would strip down and run around the house posing and shouting, "Naked girl!" "Naked boy!" "Naked girl!" "Naked boy!"

I would yell to my wife, "What's wrong with these kids? What kind of weird superhero pornography are they watching?"

"They don't watch any weird superhero pornography. What's wrong with you?" she'd always reply.

The whole thing was a little disturbing, until I realized that their prebath ritual was something *I* really needed if I was going to overcome my disappointment and live with real spiritual passion.

God created the first human, Adam, in his image, and they shared a perfect relationship. But still, God said it was *not good*. Why? Because Adam was created to love God and love people, yet at this point he was only loving God.

The solution to Adam's problem is Eve. So God created Eve, and Adam went from having a perfect relationship with God to having a perfect relationship with God *and* with Eve. And it was *good*. The Bible describes the relationship Adam and Eve shared with each other and with God by saying they were both "naked and were not ashamed."[1]

Unfortunately, what happens next for Adam and Eve is not so good. The sequence of events goes like this: (1) Adam and Eve sin. They rebel against God's one rule for them. (2) They scream, "Aaahhh! We're nudists!" (3) They start a beach volleyball team. (I may not be remembering this correctly.) (4) They cover up. In shame, they cover their nakedness from each other. For the first time, people don the T-shirt. (5) They hide from God. (6) Despite their sin, God seeks them out. (7) Adam and Eve blame each other for what happened.[2]

People always focus on the fact that this is the first time Adam and Eve's fellowship with God is broken, and obviously that is a problem. But what's often ignored is that this is the first time Adam and Eve's fellowship with *each other* is broken, and that is a problem as well. They were no longer naked. They were no longer not ashamed.

⌒

God wants me to be naked and not ashamed. He wants me to run towards people, towards relationships, with true vulnerability. Unfortunately what I tend to do is cover up, run away from others, and hide.

Why do I do this? Well, it's because Adam and Eve's story is *my* story. Because, like them, I've experienced relationships getting all messed up by sin, and I don't want to experience it again so I refuse to be vulnerable.

A couple of summers ago I had a problem with my lawnmower. A wheel kept falling off the track. Each time

I would have to stop, bend over, grab the lawnmower, put the wheel back on the track, and start the mower back up. One day I grabbed the lawnmower at the wrong place and burned my hand. It was bad. Like chargrilled, hospital trip, bandages bad. And the next few times I mowed, when the wheel fell off the track I was cautious touching the mower. I would call my kids over, "Touch this for Daddy and see if it's hot."

Growing up, I was "burned" by my father and it led me to despise him. In fact, he died about seven years ago and I was glad. There was a point in his life when my father told me he was a Christian. I doubted it. There was no evidence of it in his life. But I feared it was true. I remember thinking, *If I get to heaven and he's there, I'm leaving.*

Why did I feel that way? Because he was a harsh, critical, verbally and emotionally abusive man. He had no patience for and would not tolerate mistakes. Like one time when I was twelve, we were in a van, and he said, "Would you hand me that?" as he pointed at a pile of stuff. I grabbed what I thought he wanted and gave it to him. I guessed wrong. He was furious. He told me how stupid I was, how bad I was. Another time when I was eight we went with another family to play mini-golf. The adults were at one hole, kids at another. My little sister was taking about twenty strokes on one hole and still hadn't made it. I told her there was a limit. We had to move on. She started crying. My father came over with his putter, swung, and took out my legs. He walked away telling me how stupid I was, how bad I was.

Probably the worst moment happened when I was eight years old. I lived in New Jersey. One night I was awoken by a hand on my shoulder. It was my dad shaking me awake. "C'mon, we're moving."

I didn't understand. "What?"

"We've gotta move. Now. C'mon."

And so we loaded up a truck in the middle of the night and left New Jersey for Florida. My dad was trying to get away from some people. But I didn't care. My father and I took the truck down to Florida. My mother and sister took our car but stopped on the way to visit family, so my father and I got there first. We went out to dinner, where my dad met this lady. They talked and talked, but I didn't think anything of it. Later we went to a hotel room. I was still sad about having to move and was missing my mom and sister. My one consolation was it's cool to stay in a hotel room with your dad. But then my father told me he was going out for the night. He said not to worry. He would lock the door behind him. I shouldn't open it for anyone. And he left.

There I was alone in a hotel room. I tried to sleep, but was too afraid. Neon fingered its way through the slats of the plastic blinds, giving the room an ominous purple glow. Occasionally I would steal a look out the window, hoping I'd see my father returning but at the same time hoping he never would. Maybe he wouldn't. He had disappeared for weeks at a time in the past. But what would I do? I didn't have money. Did my mother know where I was? I tried to sleep again but my brain would not shut down. I kept thinking about losing all my friends back in New Jersey. And what would the kids be like in Florida? And how could my father leave me here?

That's when I saw the ashtray. It had been sitting on the table the whole time, but I hadn't noticed it. I shoved down the blanket, jumped off the bed, grabbed the ash-tray, carried it to the bathroom, broke it in the tub, took a shard of glass, and tried to slit my wrist.

I wasn't successful.

Then I freaked out. I was hit by an insane fear that my father would discover what I had done and go ballistic on me. So I crawled around the bathroom, frantically picking up all the pieces of glass and flushing them down the toilet. But I still spent the rest of the night imagining that if my father returned he would notice the ashtray was missing. This made no sense since my father didn't smoke, but nothing made sense to me anymore.

The only thing that made sense was my pain.

Back in bed I thought, *I don't ever want to feel this way again. I would rather not feel anything than feel this way. I'd rather be dead than experience this.* And I made a vow never to care about anything. I would not get close to friends. I would not trust my parents. I would not let anyone hurt me.

About ten years later I received a CD boom box as a graduation present. That CD player has since moved with me from dorm room to dorm room, from college to college, from apartment to house. Somewhere along the way the antenna broke off, which didn't seem like a big deal at the time because it still played CDs.

That CD boom box currently sits in my office, and it still plays CDs. However, there are times when I want to listen to the radio. Days when I want to put on my favorite station and hear the music. But I can't. All I get is static.

With that hotel-room decision never to care about anything, I broke off my antenna. Living the Jesus life means loving God and loving people, but I had become almost incapable of receiving or giving love. C. S. Lewis said that to love is to be vulnerable.[3] That night in the hotel room, I decided vulnerable is the one thing I would not be.

I was no longer naked.

I was numb.

Even as I've slowly grown in my ability to feel loved by God, I've struggled to love God in return, and especially to love people. In fact, often what I've done is just the opposite.

⁓

About twenty-five years after that hotel room experience, I was in bed again. This time I wasn't alone; my wife of then eight years was next to me. The Bible says light exposes lies, but sometimes truth comes out in the dark. It did that night. A couple of minutes after saying good night, when you're not sure whether the other person has fallen asleep, Jen said my name.

"Vince?"

I opened my eyes. "Yeah?"

"Vince, I don't like you."

I closed my eyes.

How do you respond to that? It wasn't that I didn't care. I did. But I wasn't surprised.

My father wounded me. And I, like Adam and Eve, covered up. I put walls between myself and God, and between myself and other people. It's challenging to love through a wall. Only rarely did I experience God's love, and this left me without much love to offer.

I grew up thinking I was a bad person. How could I not? I heard it all the time. I had been tattooed a bad person, and it was easier to just live it out.

I was angry. Years of suffering abuse and never doing anything with it left me seething inside. I was a Christian now, but I was a Christian with anger fantasies. I'd imagine dragging some guy who cut me off out of his car, shoving him into a microwave, and watching his head explode. Then I'd sigh and smile.

I grew up learning from my father's example. Even though I hated that part of him, I now had very little patience or tolerance when people made mistakes. I became the very thing I detested. I was never as emotionally abusive as he was, and I was never physically abusive at all, but I had a way of making people feel stupid when they screwed up.

And more than to anyone else I did this to my wife, the person I loved the most. She would tell you I'm exaggerating how bad I was, but . . . she's nice. I was not the husband I should have been. She deserved better. If she made mistakes, I let her know about it. I made it obvious that I was angry, that she never lived up to my standards.

And so, when she told me she didn't like me, it wasn't like she was first on the scene with breaking news. I already knew.

Once, when my son was four, he marched out of the bathroom, looked me in the eye, and asked, "Daddy, where does our poop go?"

What a great question! It has to go somewhere. Can you imagine if toilets didn't flush? Eventually we'd be in the bathroom sitting on a mountain of poop.

That night, in the darkness of my bedroom, I realized this was my life.

There was a reason my wife didn't like me. I was not only numb. My poisoned childhood had also left me toxic. There were things from my past that I could not forget. They were driving me away from the heart of Jesus, and I was hurting people.

For years I had toyed with the idea of getting help, but the "I don't like you" dagger finally forced me to take action. It was time for me to get drastic.

I went to counseling. Some may not think this is drastic—lots of people go to counseling—but it was drastic for me. I didn't want to go. I mean, what if someone saw me, their pastor, going to counseling? What would they guess was wrong? Or if I told them I was trying to become a better husband, how would they assume I treated my wife? I didn't want to go, but I did.

After I described my childhood, the counselor asked if I had ever tried to hold a beach ball under water in a swimming pool. I was suspicious. What did my problems have to do with beach balls? Was he trying to picture me in a swimming suit?

He explained that you can hold a beach ball under water, but it takes a lot of energy, and eventually it will pop up. He told me not dealing with my past was like that. It was sapping my energy, and the beach ball was surfacing in inappropriate anger.

Counseling helped, but not enough. (It also made me nervous about going in the pool, which I didn't appreciate.)

I had two friends who had gone to a support group called Living Waters. Living Waters started as a ministry to people who were gay but wanted to come out of their homosexual lifestyle. Later it was broadened to include people with various kinds of sexual addictions. Each of my two friends told me I should go.

I have problems, but none of them are sexual. My two friends struggled with pornography. Believe it or not, I've never seen Internet pornography. I've never seen a pornographic movie. I haven't seen a pornographic magazine since a kid showed me one in eighth grade. So when my friends told me I should go, I was thankful. Not because I wanted to go but because they had pointed out the one support group I didn't need! I'm not gay and I don't have any sexual addictions. But they explained that this support group dealt with issues of forgiveness, especially forgiving your parents. They insisted it would help me. They gave me details. The group met every Monday night, twenty-seven weeks in a row, from 7 to 10 p.m. There would be hours of reading and homework assignments to do each week.

I'm busy. I've got lots to do, and apparently I'm already using a lot of my energy keeping beach balls under water. I also have little kids I like to put in bed at night. Living Waters was the most drastic thing I could conceive of doing, and I hated the idea.

I went.

The most difficult part may have been walking in the first night. I was embarrassed that I would be the odd man out in a group of men who were battling sexual addictions. Each week when it was my turn I would need to say, "Sorry, guys, I don't deal with any of that. Thank God. Stinks to be you!" Would they want me there? Would they kick me out?

I went anyway.

The second week our group leader led us through guided prayer imagery. He asked us to close our eyes and do some visualizing.

I have to tell you: I'm just not into this kind of thing. I'm not saying it's wrong; I'm sure it's great for a lot of people, just not me. So I rolled my eyes and then closed them.

The leader asked us to imagine walking through a thick green forest to a gently flowing stream.

The leader said, "You're walking through a forest."

I thought, *At what point do the trees start singing?*

"There's a stream with a boat in it," he said. "You get in."

I thought, *How nice for me!*

"Jesus is walking towards you," he continued. "He climbs in with you."

I thought, *Rock the boat! Don't rock the boat, baby!*

He said, "Jesus looks at you for a minute, and then he opens his mouth and he speaks to you . . . what does he say?"

Whatever! I thought, *This is dumb.*

But then Jesus said something.

If you're thinking, *Please, I don't buy that kind of stuff,* I understand; I struggle with it too. I don't know if it's a gift or a curse, but it's almost impossible for me to believe in anything. Yet that night, to my surprise, I heard Jesus speak.

Jesus said, "You have a good heart, Vince."

What? I thought, *I don't know if that was Jesus talking, but if it was, it turns out Jesus is clueless! Because the one thing I know about myself is that I don't have a good heart. That's why I'm in this group, because I'm mean to people, because I make my wife feel bad.*

But Jesus said, "You have a good heart, Vince."

Those twenty-seven weeks became a debate between me and God over who was right. One night we were doing prayer time in the group. Everyone gets in a circle and puts a hand on the person being prayed for, then the leader prays out loud for him. In our group there was only one guy who struggled with same-sex attraction. Everyone else, except me, had sexual problems of a heterosexual nature. But this one guy was battling the fact that he did not want to live a homosexual life anymore. I was the only guy without any sexual problems, and that made me feel awkward, so I wondered if he felt awkward too. We were about to pray for him. He shared what we could pray for and everyone put their hand on him. Then he said, "Oh, one more thing . . ." and everyone immediately took their hands off him. I noticed that and wondered if he was sensitive to it. Did he think we didn't want to touch him because he was gay? So I put my hand back on his shoulder, and left it there. He began to tell us other things to pray for, and he went on for a long time. I thought my arm was going to fall off, but I did not take my hand off of him. Then I heard that voice: "You have a good heart, Vince."

No I don't.

"Yes you do."

Another time that same guy confessed some things during our discussion time. They were really personal, sinful, difficult things that were embarrassing to share. When he was done, the leader asked, "Does anyone have anything they want to tell him?" Total silence. Finally, I said, "I'm really proud of you . . . for being willing to share that. I'm just really proud of you." And he burst into tears. He was sobbing and cried out, "Thank you for saying that. No one has ever told me they were proud of me before."

And that voice said it again: "You have a good heart, Vince."

No I don't.

"Yes you do."

I could share more stories like this. But I'll fast-forward. After going to this group for months, I was on an airplane reading a book. The author wrote about how his whole life had been dictated by six bad memories from his childhood. He had repeatedly chosen to focus on these painful experiences. He explained how he finally decided not to focus on those anymore and instead to remember all the good things he experienced as a child. I read that paragraph and kept going. Then I read it again. *Whatever,* I thought, and kept reading. But then I read it a third time and thought, *Okay, God, I'll try it.*

So I shut the book, closed my eyes, and prayed, *God, you're going to have to help me with this. What good memories do I have of my father? What good qualities did he have? What good things did he impart?* And I started thinking and praying, and I was surprised that some stuff started to come to mind, and then some more. He was generous. He taught me to be polite. He taught me not to care about the color of a person's skin. He was funny. It began to feel like I was giving the eulogy at his funeral. This went on for about twenty minutes. When I finished, I thought, *I love my dad. I wish he was still alive. I hope he's in heaven so I can spend more time with him.* Then my head spun like vinyl in the hands of a master DJ. What was *that*? I love my *dad*? So I decided to test myself.

Oh, you love him now, huh? I said to myself. *You wish you could spend more time with him? Well, what about the time he hit you with the golf club?*

"Yeah, he definitely had problems, but I love him," I replied.

I wasn't ready to quit yet. *Well, what about the time he broke your mother's piano in the middle of the night and left?*

I answered, "Yeah, all that is true. He wasn't a good father, but still I just hope he's in heaven."

It was probably the weirdest experience of my life.

Why did it happen? Was it that I had prayed about forgiving my father for years? Was it the counseling? Was it the support group? Was it the book I was reading? Was it the airline peanuts? I don't know. Maybe it was all of that. But ever since that flight and the eulogy fantasy, I'm different. I'm not the toxic person I used to be.

Usually, I don't notice the change, but sometimes it startles me. Months after the flight I was in the parking lot of a supermarket with my family. We got to the car with our groceries and my wife started searching for her keys in her purse. Several minutes passed until finally she located them. The whole time I just stood there, then I grabbed bags and started putting them in the car. All of a sudden I realized that in the past that key thing would have driven me nuts. Beach balls would have been shooting as if launched by water cannons. But I was calm. No lecture. No mean look. No beach balls. *Who* am *I*? I thought. So I turned to my wife. "This is a weird question," I said, "but . . . have I . . . changed?"

"Changed what?" she asked.

"Changed . . . like *me*. My personality. Am I nicer . . . more patient?"

"Are you kidding? You've *totally* changed!" she said.

Another day I was doing something in the garage and my wife walked in, hugged me, and said, "It is a joy to be married to you." Then she turned around and walked out. I yelled after her, "What is *that* supposed to mean?"

In bed, the year before, I was not surprised. This time, she had shocked me. A joy to be married to *me*?

And it's not just my relationship with my wife. I have more fun playing with my kids. I cry more at movies. I laugh easier. I still struggle some with all the stuff I mentioned, but I'm not nearly so numb anymore, or toxic.

God has resurrected my antenna, and I'm picking up more than static.

I can hear the music.

Maybe things have happened in your life that have forced you to cover up, and left you feeling numb. Perhaps you've been poisoned and have become toxic. Maybe you're keeping some beach balls under water. And no, I'm not trying to picture you in your swimsuit.

Sometimes you have to revisit your past to experience God's future. And if you're living a covered-up, walled-in life, the reason you're disappointed is not because God hasn't delivered. It's because those walls keep you from loving God and people. And if you're going to live the Jesus life, you *have* to love God and love people.

What do you need to do to take off your covering and knock down your walls? Make an appointment with a counselor? Sign up for that support group? Make that difficult phone call you've been putting off? Forgive your parent? Confess your sin? Attend that AA meeting?

Maybe it's time for you to get drastic.

Maybe it's time for you to get naked.

DIE

13

The room was like bread left out on the counter for three days. The air was stale. The smell had a decaying odor. The mood was brittle. Then I saw her. I had been warned about the mask jacketing her face, imposing oxygen on her lungs. I wasn't prepared for the lack of hair, the emaciated face, the sunken chest. Her eyes were closed, and if it wasn't for the slow, steady beep of the machines I wouldn't have assumed there was life still lingering in this body. Her daughter said, "Mom, my pastor is here. Remember, we told you? We told you we were going to have him come pray for you?"

I heard something. The sound came from the vicinity of her mouth. I stared at her lips. It was barely perceptible, but they were moving. Whatever she was muttering through her parched throat and mouth, she was saying again and again. It was almost as if her groaned words were keeping time with the monotonous beeping, converging to make an ominous dirge.

I bent in to discern her words. Finally, I understood. She was moaning, over and over,

I don't want to die.
I don't want to die.
I don't want to die.

Who does? I have known only one unique soul who seemed to genuinely invite death. I met him in the summer of 1995. He was short, had brown hair, and liked to lick his butt. He was my beagle / springer spaniel mix, and this dog had a death wish. His name was Buster.

One morning my wife went to a wholesale grocery store—the kind where you can't get a 16-*ounce* jar of mayonnaise, you have to buy a 16-*pound* jar of mayonnaise—and returned with a huge tub of chocolate chunk cookies for her chocolate chunk husband. We left to run errands, placing my new prized possession on the counter. We knew that chocolate is deadly poisonous to dogs but figured Buster couldn't get up on the counter, nor could he open a sealed plastic container.

We were wrong.

Apparently, Buster had been hiding skills for years for just this moment. Somehow he got up on the counter. I like to picture the scene from *Mission: Impossible* when Tom Cruise descends into a computer room by wires attached to his waist and legs, but that's probably not how Buster did it. How he opened the container, I'll never know.

All I can say for sure is that when we arrived, the plastic tub was laying on the floor, open and empty.

I screamed, "Noooooo! My cookieeesss!"

Then I saw Buster. He came staggering into the room like some Irish guy after a St. Patrick's Day party. His stomach was bloated. It was huge—like a little kid who puts a big pillow under her shirt to make it look like she's pregnant. His face reminded me of a green olive. I said, "Buster! You ate my chunky chocolate goodness?"

I knew that chocolate is poisonous to dogs and that if they eat enough, it could kill them. I realized this could be the end for Buster, but assumed there was nothing I could do, so I thanked Jesus that at least Buster had enjoyed a great last meal, and turned on the TV. Later, I found out from a veterinarian that if your dog eats chocolate, you are supposed to make him drink hydrogen peroxide. (I also learned that if your dog drinks antifreeze, the veterinarian will pump vodka into his system for several days. I can just picture Buster, drunk out of his mind, stumbling around, "My pipes are clean!" Absolut Buster.)

I didn't know to give Buster hydrogen peroxide, so I gave him nothing. And he seemed okay, until that evening when Buster began vomiting milkshakes. Nice, thick, chocolate milkshakes. Since he couldn't digest the chocolate, his system got rid of it . . . right in the middle of my living room, and then in my bedroom, and then in my living room again. I had cleaned up Buster's vomit before, and it was always gross. But there was something different this time. I was crouched over it with a bucket and towel when I caught a whiff. It smelled great! It was pure chocolate. And it looked *tasty*. (And then I was *really* grossed out!) The good news is that Buster didn't experience death by chocolate.

Another time my wife and I smelled gas upstairs, so we had someone from the gas company come out. He went up in our bedroom, opened the window, and carefully stepped out onto the roof. He was examining our siding when Buster ran into the bedroom, saw the open window, and jumped straight out. He, of course, had no idea there was a roof out there, but landed on it anyway. Finally, the guy corralled Buster back into the house and said to me, "In the course of my job I thought I'd seen it all, but I've never seen anything like *that*. This dog has no fear of death."

A couple months later our mailman knocked on the door. I opened it, and Buster dashed out. I took chase. Buster was fast, and years of chocolate chunk cookies had slowed me to less than my former Olympic record–setting speed. The problem was that Buster was getting closer and closer to the traffic-filled main road. I screamed, "Buster, you're gonna get hit!" But years of chocolate chunk cookies had slowed Buster's brain to less than his former Mensa record–setting intelligence. Finally, right near the road . . . Buster squatted. I thought, *This is my last chance to grab him.* I sprinted for Buster, who saw my move and took off. Oddly, he was still squatting, still doing his business, as he made his escape. He ran directly into the road. I thought, *Oh crap!* (which now seems especially appropriate considering the circumstances of that moment). A motorcycle swerved and just missed him. A car came barreling right at him. What I will remember forever are the sounds that followed.

The lady in the car shrieked. I could hear the scream through her closed windows.

Aaaaaahhhhhh!

She slammed the brakes.

Eeeeerrrrrrrrr

The next noise I heard was the car hitting Buster. It was like the sound of a NFL linebacker making a vicious tackle.

Thuummpfff

The next noise came out of Buster. It was a sound that could only rise out of an animal that belonged in the wild.

Aaarrrewwweeehhhooo

That's it, I thought. *He finally got what he wanted. He's dead.*

Then I saw something I'll never forget—a brown blur of fur. Buster had jumped up . . . and ran past me at full speed. I couldn't believe he was alive, let alone could move and could move that *fast*. I yelled, "Buster!" and, finally, he stopped, turned, and gave me a dazed look, like, "Did you get the license plate number?"

Buster had a death wish.

But most of us, like the woman in the hospital, don't want to die. And that seems normal enough, but there's a problem with it. The problem is that real living comes through dying. Jesus said, "If anyone would come after me, he must deny himself and take up his cross and follow me. For whoever wants to save his life will lose it, but whoever loses his life for me and for the gospel will save it."[1] A life of following Jesus is a life of taking up a cross. In his time only one kind of person took up a cross, someone on their way to crucifixion. Condemned criminals were forced to carry their own crosses to the place of execution.

To follow Jesus is to choose self-execution. It's to choose death.

Followers of Jesus crucify their egocentric desires so they can live for God and others. Instead of "I don't want to die," they live for death. Moment by moment, choice by choice, they die to themselves and live for others.

We should be grasping at death, not life.

Jesus didn't just tell us about this, he modeled it. Not only in the big things, like literally carrying a cross and dying on it for us, but also in the moment-by-moment, choice-by-choice, daily parts of life. Like the time Jesus washed his disciples' feet.

If you lived in Jesus' time, you'd have walked around in sandals on dusty, unpaved streets. Pretty quickly your feet would become caked in mud, sweat, or perhaps some animal droppings you hadn't noticed. There was a custom that if you had friends over, you would have a servant or one of your children wash their feet as they entered your home.

The foot washer was the lowest man on the totem pole. And it had to be one of the worst jobs of all time, because feet are nasty. Some people have a thing for feet, but I don't understand that. There is *nothing* good about feet. For instance, compare hands and feet. Many good things can be said about or done with hands. "You have a firm handshake." "Thumbs up!" There's a whole language based on hands—sign language. Back in the '80s, "Hands Across America" brought thousands of people together to hold hands. In the '90s Jewel sang, "These hands are small I know, but they are not yours, they are my own." Way back in the '60s the Beatles sang, "I want to hold your hand." At concerts, audiences are told to "throw your hands up in the air—and wave 'em like you just don't care." And then there's the greatest all-time song about hands . . . Neil Diamond . . . "Hands, touchin' hands, reachin' out touchin' me, Sweet Caroline."

Feet are the opposite. What can you say? "Hey, your feet smell great today!" "Oh, I love what you've done with the hair on your feet. Did you just get a perm?" "Your feet are so beautiful, is that their natural color?" "Just between us girls, are those feet real, or did you have surgery?" And what if sign language were done with feet? It wouldn't work. And if it were "Feet Across America," it wouldn't have been thousands of people, it would have been three or four sickos out in a field trying to clasp bare feet. And what if those songs were about feet? "These feet are small I know, but they are not yours, they are my own." "I want to hold your foot." "Throw your feet up in the air—and wave 'em like you just don't care." "Feet, touchin' feet, reachin' out touchin' me . . . Please get your stinkin' feet off of me!"

There is nothing positive to say about feet. Feet are nasty, which is why the foot washer was the lowest man on the totem pole. (The next lowest man on the totem pole, if you're wondering, was the town's elephant proctologist.)

So one night Jesus had a dinner party with his twelve closest followers. Everything was arranged, except there was no foot washer. Everyone knew this was a job fit for a lowly servant, for the person with the lowest standing. And so Jesus' twelve friends looked anxiously at each other, making "I'm not going to do it" eyes and "I know I'm more important than you" gestures. Finally, the meal was served, but the feet were still filthy.

Then, as everyone ate, Jesus stood up, grabbed a towel and basin and began washing his friends' feet. A fog of uncomfortable silence must have descended on the room. Not only did the twelve apprentices of Jesus feel embarrassed, they were also probably confused. Why was Jesus lowering himself to such a level? Did he understand that he was taking the role of a slave?

What *they* didn't understand was that he was demonstrating for them the Jesus life, which is a life of grasping at death. It's a life of dying to our own selfish needs and putting others first.

Finally, Jesus finished drying the last foot. He stood up and spoke, "Now that I, your Lord and Teacher, have washed your feet, you also should wash one another's feet. I have set you an example that you should do as I have done for you. I tell you the truth, no servant is greater than his master, nor is a messenger greater than the one who sent him. Now that you know these things, you will be blessed if you do them."[2]

Jesus says you must do as I have done. Don't seek your own happiness; instead, serve others. Walk into every situation looking for how you can help others, rather than seeking to promote your own interests. Moment by moment, choice by choice, choose death.

And then he closes by saying, "Now that you know these things, you will be *blessed* if you do them." He was telling us, "If you choose death, you will find life. Real life. The life you're missing out on but desperately want."

Living the Jesus life means choosing death. The problem is, like that woman in the hospital, we don't want to die. I know I don't. It just seems too risky. Just the thought of abandoning myself to a life of choosing death fills my head with questions.

But if I deny myself, how will I be happy?

If I don't look after myself, who will look after me?

If I'm always putting others first, what if they start taking advantage of me?

So does this mean I can never do what I want to do?

How will I have any more fun?

The truth is I often live my life as a worship service to me. I strive to meet *my* needs and wants. One of my biggest wants is to be comfortable. And so I grasp at that.

I even have a throne. I bought it about a year ago. It's a La-Z-Boy chair. For years I'd dreamed of owning an easy chair but could never afford one. Then I came across one on sale. It was 50 percent off the *sale price*. It wasn't the best quality chair, but for 50 percent off the sale price I'd buy a chair made of stone and upholstered in sandpaper. (I have some toilet paper made of sandpaper. Not nearly as soothing as other brands, but it too was 50 percent off the sale price. I almost ordered a mail-order bride once, because she was 50 percent off the sale price, but my wife had some kind of problem with it.) This chair is ridiculously comfortable. You sink into it, pull the lever lifting the footrest, lean it back into the recline mode, and become a picture of relaxation. Put a crown on me and I am the king of comfortable. But here's what I've discovered about this chair: it's the easiest place in the house to fall asleep.

And what I've been learning is that the same holds true in life. When I devote myself to being a lazy boy in an easy chair I may be comfortable, but I'm also spending my life asleep. I never experience life fully awake. I am comfortable but also bored and disappointed.

See, easy chairs are great for taking naps and watching exhilarating things happen on TV, but nothing exciting ever happens to a person sitting in one. I checked—no game-winning touchdown pass has ever been caught by a guy sitting in a La-Z-Boy. No buzzer-beating, three-point shot has ever been made by a guy sitting in a La-Z-Boy. And no action adventure movie has ever featured a character sitting in a La-Z-Boy. Can you picture *Die Hard . . . in an Easy Chair*? Or *Terminator 4: The Lazy Boy*? Or how about *Indiana Jones and the Temple of Soft Cushiony Leather*?

When I make my comfort preeminent and am content to relax in the easy chair, I nap while others are involved in the action. I watch TV while others live the adventure.

I think it's too risky to move out of my comfort zone and serve others rather than myself, but the riskiest thing is to remain in the chair. In the chair I grasp at life and come up with death. It's only when I leave the chair and grasp at death that I find life.

Now it's easy for me to say that I need to get into action this instant, and I know it's right, but the reality is that I am repeatedly pulled away from that truth. I live in a world where I'm constantly bombarded with messages that teach the opposite, and it's hard not to listen. The world says the path to true happiness and the greatest possible joy is to serve self. Look out for number one and get as much as you can. The faster car you have, the happier you'll be. The bigger house you have, the happier you'll be. The nicer clothes you have, the happier you'll be. The larger your bank account, the happier you'll be. Whoever dies with the most toys wins. Want to have a great night? Eat food *you* want to eat. Pick a movie *you* want to watch. Hang out with people *you* want to spend time with. That's the way to experience real life.

But then there's the voice of Jesus telling me, "No, that's the path to death. If you want to really live, you must choose death. You must live for and serve others." Jesus says the path to true happiness and the greatest possible joy is to serve *others*. You need to look out for everyone else and give away as much as you can. The slower car you have, the happier you'll be. The smaller house you have, the happier you'll be. The worse the clothes, the smaller the bank account—whoever dies with the *least* toys wins. (Try marketing that bumper sticker!)

Every summer at our church dozens of people go on short-term mission trips. When they return, they rave, "It was incredible! I had the greatest time! It was probably the best experience of my life!" And people think it's because of *where* they were. They say, "God's really moving in Laos! He's doing incredible things *over there*!" They say, "Man, Costa Rica's so beautiful! It's incredible *over there*!" They say, "If I lived in Haiti, I'd be close to

God all the time; my life would be so much simpler and better—it would be incredible *over there!*"

But they're wrong.

It's not about *where* they were; it's about what they were *doing*. What they experienced was not due to a change of geography but to a change of heart. For a week all they did was wash feet. They left their easy chairs in America, flew to another country, and *served*. They didn't think about getting a faster car, bigger house, nicer clothes, or a larger bank account. They didn't get to choose what they wanted for dinner, they ate what was given to them—and sometimes it was disgusting. They didn't pick out their entertainment for the evening; there was *no* entertainment for the evening. They didn't hang out with their fun friends; they hung out with the poor— people they probably wouldn't have given a second glance at home. And that was the best time of their life?

Yes.

The Jesus life is lived by people who choose to die by serving others rather than themselves.

I'll be honest. When I first came into Christianity, I couldn't believe how self-consumed and comfort-obsessed Christians were. I wondered if we were reading the same Bible. Had they ignored the verses where Jesus said to carry a cross, to die to self, to choose death? Had they missed the story about washing feet?

But, over time, I have seen the same self-obsession and comfort-addiction creep into my own life. Often I'm able to conveniently ignore noticing this, but every once in a while I get smacked in the face with it.

Like a few years ago my friend Mark and his family moved to Laos to do mission work there. And I thought, *Could I do that? If I really believed God wanted me to up and move to Laos, would I do it?* I thought, *Of course I would*, but I had my doubts. Then, before this family left, I told them that I would come over to see them on a church mission trip. They laughed and said, "We'll believe that when we see it!" And I realized, *Wait a second, I'm wondering if I would move there, but apparently there is something about me that makes people question if I'd even be willing to go there for two weeks! What is that? Do they know about my King of Comfort crown? Have they seen this lazy boy sleeping in his easy chair?*

Now that we had missionaries established in Laos, I started praying for Vietnam. We had committed to try and reach a people group that lived in several Asian countries. So I repeatedly prayed that God would give me some way into Communist-ruled Vietnam and at least get my foot in the door there. After praying that for a few years, I received an email one day. It was from a pastor I had met just once. He wrote, "Hey, Vince, I'm going to Vietnam to meet with government officials. They told me I could bring some pastors from other churches who might want to help their country and you came to mind. Want to go?"

My first thought was, *No!* As I mentioned earlier, the trip was fifteen days long. My family had a vacation planned for seven of those days. I would miss my daughter's first day of kindergarten.

Then I realized: God had just answered my prayers in nothing less than miraculous fashion. I had a once-in-a-lifetime opportunity staring at me, and saying yes could potentially lead to years of being able to do ministry in a Communist country where Christianity is basically illegal—and I'm going to say no because it would interrupt my plans?

I went.

About a year ago I had another experience like this one. I was asked to help with a new church start in Cleveland.

I was to be on a "Management Team"—giving advice and coaching to the guy starting the church. I agreed and then found out I'd have to fly to Cleveland for a day of meetings. This did not make the King of Comfort happy. Airplanes don't have La-Z-Boy chairs. Cleveland is much colder than where I live. I'd have to be away from my family.

But I went.

After the meetings someone drove me to the airport in Cleveland to catch my return flight. I was early, so I sat down at my gate to read a book. I was in the middle of reading when the most unforgettable sensory experience of my life occurred. I was suddenly hit by a smell . . . I don't have words to describe it.

Repulsive.

Disgusting.

Revolting.

Foul.

Nauseating.

None of those words do this smell justice. I'm serious.

I instantly started gagging. I tried to figure out the source of the smell, but couldn't, and slowly it faded away. I went back to reading, but then the smell attacked me again. Holding my breath and trying not to retch, I looked and saw a woman who had just walked up. From her physical appearance and dress it was obvious she was from the Middle East. I gave her a quick once over and realized the problem. She was wearing sandals. She carried a thin plastic grocery bag that contained sneakers. Only sneakers. The smell was coming from her feet, or perhaps her sandals and sneakers. She had decided to stand right next to me, and I couldn't hold my breath any longer.

In that moment I started having this rapid-fire inner dialogue. . .

This is the most sickening experience of my life.

Vince, chill out. She's a person, she is not her smell.

149

She may be a person, but she doesn't smell like one.
Vince, she's from the Middle East. They eat different foods from you. Those foods have certain smells. And maybe she's been walking all day. So her feet are sweaty. It's not a big deal.

Not a big deal? I am getting up, and getting out of here!

Vince, don't you walk away from her!

She won't know why I'm walking away from her. It won't insult her.

No, Vince, don't walk away, even if she doesn't know, even if it doesn't insult her. This isn't about her, it's about you.

Exactly, this is about *me*. That's why *I'm* getting out of here. I am not comfortable sitting here.

Vince, maybe the most important thing isn't for you to be comfortable. Maybe it's for you to put another person first. Maybe the best thing would be for you to be uncomfortable.

That's stupid. Sitting next to her isn't putting her first anyway. It's not like I'm going to talk to her or start a friendship with her. So it's no big deal if I'm not around her. I'm leaving.

Vince, don't leave. This is your chance to grasp death and experience real *life.*

No, I'm leaving. Talk about death—it's going to kill me if I stay here one more second!

But Vince, what if not staying here kills your soul?

Whatever. I'm leaving.

And I did. I got up, very subtly, and I walked away. I walked as far away as I could, and then started gulping for air like someone who had been held under water for three minutes. I found a place on the floor to sit down, and I went back to reading my book. Finally the announcement came that my flight was boarding, so I walked over to the line. Seconds later I was assaulted by the stench. I turned around and found that the woman, and her sandals and sneakers, were right behind me. I tried to fake a smile at her, turned back around, and thought, *Yeah, that's funny, God. You have a great sense of humor.*

As we waited to board, and then finally entered the plane, I tried to take as few breaths as possible, and only through my mouth. Then I realized: she might be sitting near me on the plane! I started frantically praying, *God, I know this is wrong. I know. I know. I know. But please, please, don't let her be sitting next to me.*

She sat next to me.

I was on the aisle, 19C. She was just across the aisle, 19D.

Unbelievable!

I started grumbling inside, *I can't believe this. I come all the way to Cleveland out of the goodness of my heart to help this guy with a church he's starting and look what I get. I shouldn't have even come. I should have just stayed home. I can't believe I have to sit next to this Middle Eastern woman who smells like whatever gross thing it is Middle Eastern people eat, and next to her vile smelling feet and sandals. How far did this woman walk today anyway? Has she heard of soap and water?*

And then it hit me . . .

Jesus was from the Middle East.

Jesus ate whatever it is Middle Eastern people eat.

Jesus walked all day, every day.

Jesus wore sandals.

Jesus rarely would have had soap touch his feet.

And I realized . . . I would be offended by Jesus.

Like most Christians, I like to imagine meeting Jesus, in the flesh, and I picture myself running up to him and hugging him. But what if I ran up . . . and gagged? What if the smell coming from Jesus' feet and sandals was repulsive . . . disgusting . . . revolting . . . foul . . . nauseating? And why wouldn't it be? Why would Jesus smell any better than this woman?

It was a slap in the face. I finally understood. I was so addicted to my own comfort, so unwilling to die, that not only was it keeping me from living the Jesus life; it kept me from Jesus.

Way more than we'd like to admit, our lives are designed to be worship services to ourselves instead of God.

We wear the crown.

We grasp at life, only to come up with death.

Remember the woman in the hospital who kept whispering, "I don't want to die"? She died. Buster, my dog, didn't die from eating chocolate, jumping out the window, or getting hit by a car. But eventually he died too.

And you and I will die someday as well.

The question is, are we willing to die before we die? If not, we'll never really live.

People who grasp at life find death, but those who grasp at death find life.

It's time to die.

TOUCH

14

As homeless weddings go, the first one I performed was pretty uneventful. My second homeless wedding, however, was wild. The homeless couple was getting married in the small living room of their friend's house on Valentine's Day. I arrived about twenty minutes early. The wedding began forty minutes late. After sitting around for an hour, I de-wedged myself from between the other two people on the couch and announced, "Okaayy, we're gonna get started!"

A friend of the homeless couple said she made a special CD for the occasion and asked if she could play it. I told her that would be great. She walked over to the entertainment center. One shelf held a CD player, the other a DVD player. She dropped the CD into the DVD player. I opened my mouth to tell her she made a mistake, but music started pumping out of the speakers. It was a beautiful classical song. The lady smiled . . . and cranked it. A minute later the bride walked in. She looked around at the twenty or so people packed into the room, stared down at the floor, and nervously made her way to the groom, who was sitting in his wheelchair.

Everyone looked at me, waiting for me to speak, but I thought I should wait for the song to end. Finally it did, which was when the second song started. It was a country love ballad, I think by Faith Hill or Shania Twain. I assumed someone would realize weddings are not typically set to music and turn it off, but no one did. I hoped someone would at least turn it *down*, but that didn't happen either. Tired of everyone staring at me, I decided I shouldn't wait any longer. I *shouted*, "On behalf of Bart and Ginny, I want to welcome everyone and say how excited I am to be a part of one of the greatest days of their lives, as they give themselves to each other in marriage."

During the wedding one overly excited friend designated herself the photographer. That would have been fine, except her idea of a close-up was sticking the camera six inches from my face and snapping shots. I fought through the temporary blindness from the flash and shouted the vows.

Throughout the wedding, every three to four minutes, the song on the CD would change. This made me nervous, but most of the songs were reasonably appropriate. Finally the bride and groom kissed, turned to face the audience, and I yelled over the music, "By the power invested in me by the Commonwealth of Virginia, I present to you Mr. and Mrs. Bart and Ginny Carr."

Normally, this is the point where the couple walks out, but this couple had nowhere to go, so I shouted, "Why don't you all come up and give them a hug!" At that precise second the song on the CD changed. And, as all of Bart and Ginny's friends jumped up to embrace the newlyweds, the speakers pumped out: "The devil went down to Georgia, he was looking for a soul to steal. He was in a bind 'cos he was way behind: he was willin' to make a deal."

I started laughing.

My friend Dallas ran over to the entertainment center and turned down the volume on the *CD* player. Fortunately (for me), the CD was in the *DVD* player. The song kept playing.

I almost fell over laughing. Dallas was confused. He hit the power button on the CD player. The song kept playing.

Dallas looked helplessly over at me, but I wasn't about to tell him.

By this point homeless people started to join in and sing along in celebration: "Now you play a pretty good fiddle, boy, but give the devil his due: I bet a fiddle of gold against your soul, 'cos I think I'm better than you."

I laughed so hard I almost threw up.

My friend Dallas is the reason I perform weddings for the homeless.

About seven years ago, Dallas' wife dragged him to our church. Ever since they started dating, she'd make him go with her to a different church each Easter and Christmas, hoping something might stick. Our church was the first that connected with him. He started coming regularly with his family. About a year later, God broke through. Dallas decided to follow Jesus.

One Sunday the following year our message was about God's love for the poor and how he commands his people to take care of those who can't take care of themselves. We explained that one of the greatest needs of the homeless is shoes. We had considered asking everyone to bring shoes to donate the following Sunday but knew this would lead people to bring in their worst shoes. So immediately after the message we surprised everyone by asking them to take off the shoes they were wearing, and to leave them as a donation. We collected over four hundred pairs of shoes and gave them to a homeless mission the next day.

Dallas and his wife, Anne, were two of the people who left shoes. They went home talking about how it was one of the coolest things they had ever done but that it wasn't enough. So they made some sandwiches and took them down to the beach, hoping to find some homeless people. They did the same the following Sunday, and the Sunday after that. Soon word got out that this crazy couple was bringing food and looking for homeless people, so the homeless people started looking for them. Eventually, Dallas told everyone he would meet them at a park near the beach at 5:00 every Sunday evening. About a hundred homeless people started gathering and waiting for Dallas each week. Other people from our church started joining Dallas, adding clothes, hygiene products, medical care, and counseling.

At the time, Dallas was an upper-level manager at General Electric. But as the ministry grew Dallas left his job and gave his full-time attention to caring for the homeless. His family sold their house and moved into something much smaller. And Dallas now runs the "PIN (People in Need) Ministry" full-time.*

Dallas is one of the fastest-growing Christians I've ever met. While I come across many Christians who just seem disappointed, that would be one of the last words I'd use to describe Dallas. He's not bored to death. He's really living life fully alive.

⌣

A few years ago I was walking through an art museum, turned a corner, and had my breath taken away. It wasn't a statue. It wasn't a painting. It wasn't an exhibit. It was

*For more info (or to donate to a great cause), check out www.PIN ministry.org.

the *sign* over an exhibit. The sign read: "Touch Me I'm Sick."

It hung above the entrance to a traveling display which featured photographs from Charles Peterson. Peterson was at the epicenter of the birth of grunge music in Seattle in the late 1980s and early '90s. Mostly the exhibit contained old pictures of before-they-were-famous grunge bands like Nirvana, Pearl Jam, and Soundgarden. As a fan of grunge music, I appreciated the pictures.

But I found myself walking over and staring again and again at the name of the exhibit: "Touch Me I'm Sick." I learned that it was inspired by a song title from the band Mudhoney. I studied the photographs of Mudhoney, looking for some clue to what enabled them to so succinctly capture what I believe is the human condition.

I think the name of that exhibit is the silent cry of every person on the planet. Our problem is that we all know ourselves. I can't see inside of you, but I do know how repulsive I can be on the inside. I know how even the best things I do can be corrupted by selfish motives. I know how ugly my thoughts can become. I see the inside of me. And you see the inside of you. And we know that deep down we are sick.

And so we yearn. We crave compassion. That someone would understand and still care. We ache for healing. We long for contact. Not just the feel of skin on our skin but the caress of compassion, a hand that can bring healing. We all echo those words: Touch me, I'm sick.

⌒

Jesus came as a response to that cry. He came to touch the sick and heal them. One of the most striking examples of this is in Mark 1. Mark begins the story, "A man with leprosy came to him."[1] At the time lepers were considered human pollution. They were rejected from society and banished to live in leper colonies. When in the vicinity of nonleprous people, they had to shout, "Unclean! Unclean!"[2]

Mark doesn't provide the background behind this man's action, but sheer desperation must have erupted into extraordinary courage the day this leper decided to approach Jesus. As he came near, he probably hid behind trees to avoid the fear-induced shrieks of panic his appearance would have provoked from all who saw him.

"A man with leprosy came to him," Mark writes, "and begged on his knees, 'If you are willing, you can make me clean.'"[3] I find it fascinating that the leper didn't say, "If you are *able*, you can make me clean," but instead, "If you are *willing*." He didn't doubt Jesus' capacity to do a miracle, only his compassion.

We know how repulsive we can be on the inside, but he had become repulsive on the outside. Our motives are sometimes corrupted; his flesh had become corrupted. Our thoughts can be ugly, but this leper's skin had become ugly. Our problems are buried inside, but this man's problems had oozed out of him and taken over his body for all to see. That day he gave voice to our silent cry. He ran up to Jesus, dropped to his knees, and pleaded, "Touch me, I'm sick."

Mark concludes, "Filled with compassion, Jesus reached out his hand and touched the man, 'I am willing,' he said. 'Be clean!' Immediately the leprosy left him and he was cured."[4] Somehow this leper had heard about Jesus' power but not his character. If he had, he *never* would have doubted Jesus' compassion or his willingness to place his hand on the ailing. Because that's why Jesus came. He came to touch the sick, to infect them with his wellness.

This is why Dallas is one of the least disappointed, most effervescent and dynamic Christians I know. It's because he is living the Jesus life, and the Jesus life is all about touching the sick.

I realize that when we think about living the Jesus life, touching the sick may not be the first thing that comes to mind. But perhaps that's why so many of us are living disappointed Christian lives. At its core, the life Jesus lived and offers to us is about touching the sick, and we ignore that.

Think about this: if you had watched Jesus live his life here on earth, and then were asked to describe what living "the Jesus life" would look like, what do you think you'd say? Over seventy-five times the Gospels mention Jesus healing the sick. If you had witnessed each of those, is there any way that touching the sick *wouldn't* have been one of the main features in your description of the Jesus life?

In fact, when a man questioned whether Jesus was the real deal, Jesus sends him a message "proving" that he is. What is the message? Basically Jesus says, "Tell him that I touch the sick."[5]

And when Jesus sent his disciples out, what did he send them out to do? It was to touch the sick.[6]

Let's imagine Jesus sent his disciples out with orders to touch the sick, but they *didn't*. They went out on their journeys but never noticed those who were ailing; instead they lacked compassion for the needy, they weren't willing to reach out their hand to the ill. When they returned, would we expect them to be bubbling about how great this following Jesus thing really is *or* would we expect them to come back feeling like something was missing and perhaps even feeling a little ashamed that they hadn't obeyed?

If we're supposed to be like Jesus, shouldn't touching the sick be one of the main features of our lives? And if he's sent us out to touch the sick and we aren't, wouldn't that explain why we still feel like something is missing from our lives and why we may even feel a little ashamed?

It's time for us to live the Jesus life. It's time for us to touch the sick. And when we do, we'll start to find what we've been searching for.

⌒

The poster child in our era for touching the sick is Mother Teresa. Mother Teresa spent her life in the gutters of Calcutta, India, bathing lepers and holding the hands of the dying. And when we hear that we think, *It's nice that she served the poorest of the poor and washed lepers in the slums of Calcutta. It's noble, but it must have been a depressing life, constantly being around sickness and always having to put others first.*

Mother Teresa admitted, in personal letters and journal entries, that she underwent intense internal spiritual struggles in her relationship with God.[7] But in terms of what she chose to do every day, in ministering to the needy in India, it was just the opposite. People who knew or interviewed Mother Teresa noted that she was the most *joyful* person they ever met. One journalist wrote of Mother Teresa and her missionaries of charity, "Their life is tough and austere by worldly standards; yet I have never in my life met such delightful, happy servants, or seen such an atmosphere of *joy* as they create."[8]

Once a Muslim cleric came and watched for the longest time as Mother Teresa washed a leper. He said afterward, "All these years, I have believed that Jesus was a prophet. But today I believe Jesus Christ is God, if he is able to give such *joy* to this sister, enabling her to do her work with so much love."[9]

So what is it that inspires people like Dallas and Momma T to touch the sick? I think they understand something many of us don't. I read an interview with

Mother Teresa in *Time* magazine where she explains that the poor, the outcast, and the dying are really "Jesus in disguise." When asked what she provided for those who come to see her work, she responded, "A chance to come out and touch the poor." And she told the journalist that the poor are God's greatest gift to her, because through them she had the "opportunity to be 24 hours a day with Jesus."[10]

I asked my friend Dallas* about his experiences in touching the sick. He told me about this homeless woman named Tasha. Tasha is addicted to drugs and has a boyfriend who beats her. One evening Dallas was at a Wendy's down by the oceanfront, helping a homeless musician put together flyers, when Tasha came running in. Out of breath she gasped, "Mr. Dallas, Mr. Dallas, I need five dollars for a hotel room. Could you please help me?" Dallas could tell she hadn't eaten for a while, and she admitted it had been more than a day. So he bought her dinner, and the three of them sat together as Tasha ate. When she finished, they walked to the hotel. Tasha told the clerk, "I have all the money I need except five dollars, and Dallas here is going to pay that." Dallas paid the five dollars, Tasha thanked him, and Dallas left the hotel.

Dallas told me that when he left he was overwhelmed by a profound sense that he'd just experienced what he calls a "Matthew 25:40 moment." In Matthew 25:40 Jesus says, "I tell you the truth, whatever you did for the least of these brothers of mine, you did for me." If you had asked the hotel clerk what had just happened, she would tell you that Dallas paid five dollars to help out a homeless woman named Tasha. But, according to Dallas, he had just put Jesus in a hotel room on a cold night.

*Dallas is a fan of the Dallas Cowboys. Unbelievable! That'd be like if my friend Milwaukee Jones was a fan of the Milwaukee Brewers. (I don't actually have a friend named Milwaukee Jones, but if I did, and he liked the Brewers, that would be the same.)

The motivation for touching the sick is seeing the sick as Jesus himself. Jesus taught us that whatever we do "for the least of these," we do for him. So, in a strange twist, by living the Jesus life, we get to live life with Jesus.

⌒

I have learned from Dallas that if I want to do something for Jesus, I need to touch the sick. Now, there are no lepers in most of our neighborhoods, so that is not an option for us. But there are still all kinds of opportunities for us to touch the sick:

- Loving the unlovable. Being the one person who is willing to befriend that socially awkward person everyone avoids.
- Encouraging the depressed. Seminars and books talk about people who give us energy versus people who sap our energy, and they advise us to avoid people who are energy leeches. But perhaps if you tried to be an encouraging presence in that depressed person's life, you would infect him with your wellness, rather than him contaminating (and draining) you with his illness.
- Treating your waitress (or your garbage man, or the clerk at the store) like a person who matters, rather than reducing her to someone who simply exists to serve you.
- Sitting next to the lonely. Perhaps you could make a commitment that you will not sit next to your friends in church each Sunday but will instead look for someone who is alone.
- Finding out which incurable patients in the hospital get no visitors and showing up in their room once or twice a week with a smile and some cookies.

There are all kinds of opportunities for us to touch the sick, and when we do, we overcome our own disappointment and start to enjoy the Jesus life.

Some of my more exhilarating chances to touch the sick have come from knowing Dallas and volunteering with PIN Ministry projects. Last year on Christmas Day we threw a banquet for homeless people. A family in our church owns an awesome banquet facility. So we got some money and volunteers and buses together and planned a party. The buses picked up the homeless down by the oceanfront. We served them appetizers and hot drinks as they waited for the bus. Then we drove them over to the banquet facility. They walked in and saw fine china, cloth napkins, an elegant meal, and nice music. The looks on their faces were priceless. After dinner, as they left to board the buses, we handed each person a bag full of Christmas gifts. We also gave every child a new winter coat. People left in tears, saying they had never experienced anything like this. It was ridiculously cool.

Somehow the news heard about our banquet and a reporter showed up from the local paper. He explained that it would be the cover story of the local news section the following day. I went home that night on a high. In fact, I was so pumped about it that the next morning I got up early to drive out and get the paper. I also needed gas, so I pulled up, put the nozzle in, and walked away as it was filling up. I have never left my car as it was filling up with gas, but I was so excited to read the article and relive my experience from the night before. So I bought the paper, opened it up, found the article, and read it as I walked back to my car. I jumped in, started the car, and pulled away. Then I heard a sound. It was a loud thud, followed by a metallic scraping noise. I looked back and realized that, in my excitement, I had not taken the nozzle out of my gas tank. As I drove away, the nozzle and the entire hose had ripped out and I was dragging them behind me. I jumped out of my car and took in the disaster I had created. I looked up and saw a guy staring at me, shaking his head like, *You are the dumbest person I have ever seen in my life.* I said, "Dude! You should have been at this banquet we did yesterday for homeless people! Here, read this article!"

Thinking back on that, I have to ask myself, how often am I so excited about something that I lose track of everything else?

Just about never.

So what was it that filled me with that kind of joy?

Touching the sick.

⌒

One of the coolest examples I've ever seen of Christians touching the sick and infecting them with their wellness happened a few summers ago. I was scheduled to speak one night at a conference for teenagers in Tennessee. I flew into Tennessee and was picked up and driven to a college dorm that I'd be staying in. I walked in and there was a group of teenagers standing there talking, but the first person I saw was a boy who had no arms and no legs, and he was, well, standing—just kind of balancing there. And it took me aback. Obviously, I wasn't expecting to see that. So I smiled and tried not to give him a weird look. As I went to my room the whole way I was thinking about that kid.

Who brought him?

How had he become friends with that group he was with?

What was it about the other teenagers in that group that led them to hang out with a handicapped kid?

So I went to my room and that night I spoke to all the teenagers. At the end I was supposed to do an altar call, inviting kids who wanted to become Christians to come forward. So I gave the altar call, but because the teenagers were coming forward to their youth ministers, there was nothing for me to do. So I just stood awkwardly on the side of the stage as the band played and dozens of kids came forward. Finally, the stream of kids ended, but the band kept playing, so now I felt *really* weird. Anyway, I closed my eyes and prayed, not because I'm so spiritual but because I didn't know what else to do with myself. I prayed, *Um, God, maybe there's one more kid who's ready to give their heart to you. No one's coming forward now, but maybe there's one more kid* . . . And I opened my eyes . . . and the boy with no arms and no legs was getting pushed to the front of the room in his wheelchair by two of his friends, both with smiles beaming.

Wow, I thought, *that kid must have such a rough life. I am so glad that he's now going to have Jesus in his life. And thank you, God, that he had friends who were willing to invite him to come along, to hang out with him, to touch the sick.*

I want to be like those kids.

I need to touch the sick.

MISSION

15

Imagine one night your phone rings, disturbing you from your third straight hour of watching TV. You debate whether it's worth the energy to reach over and pick up the cordless. Finally, you grab the phone but don't recognize the number on the caller ID. Annoyed at the disturbance you push the answer button. "What?"

The voice on the other end explains that the government has chosen you to be a new special operative. After several rounds of "Very funny. Is that you Phil? Wait, is this Chris?" you finally come to believe this is truly a rep from a government agency. You challenge the sanity of their decision, but the man explains that they know what they're doing, and they want you. He needs an answer. Now.

Your mind races with all you may have to give up to take on this assignment: sleeping 'til the last minute in your comfy bed, your specialty coffee on the way into work, the Danish pastries in the kitchenette at the office, forwarding email stories to your friends during the morning work hours, the lunch debate between McDonald's or Wendy's (Meal #2 or #3?), surfing the Net at work, listening to your favorite radio talk show on the way home, and, of course, the four to five hours of TV at night. It's a lot to give up. But you decide this is the chance of a lifetime. Who knows when the government might call again? You ask, "You're talking . . . like . . . 007 stuff?"

"Yes" is the impatient reply.

"Okay, I'll do it. Sign me up. But, let me ask, the hotels I'll be staying in when I'm the road . . . they will have cable TV, right?"

The next day you start getting excited. You look through your closet to pick out your outfit for this new role. You select your best suit, put it on, and realize it has suddenly become very difficult to breathe. You haven't worn the suit in two years, and apparently you've gained twenty pounds. Realizing that breathing might be necessary for fighting crime and saving the world, you take the suit off. It wasn't nice enough anyway. You drive over to the mall, the nice mall, and rent an Armani tux. Now you look the part.

Six days later you find yourself in a casino. Realizing that slot machines are too lame for 007s and unsure of the rules of Baccarat, you decide to just saunter over to the bar and order a Coke. As it erupts all over your tux you regret ordering it "shaken, not stirred."

Soon you have objectives to accomplish. You discover that time is of the essence. You have to keep your identity secret to some but reveal it to others. Danger is in the air. So how do you feel? Nervous? Probably. Intimidated? Perhaps. Anxious? Sure. Excited? Definitely.

Bored?

No way.

⌒

Before leaving earth, Jesus spoke to his followers, "I have chosen you. You will be my secret agents. I am sending you into the world with a mission. You have objectives to accomplish. Time is of the essence. There may be strategic moments where you have to conceal your identity. Danger will surround your life. Now go."[1]

And so the obvious question is . . .

How is it that we've ended up bored?

I was twenty years old and brand new to Christianity when I became a follower of Jesus. I immediately took to Jesus' call to be his secret agent man. I rented the tux and dove headfirst into his mission.

I began sharing my new faith with friends and coworkers. Some listened attentively, others rolled their eyes; one started cursing at me and calling me names accompanied by threatening gestures. It was weird but also the most fun I had ever had.

I was Bond. James Bond.

A few months later I was on a bus in Washington DC. I was doing an internship at a government law office. My fellow intern Dan and I took the bus from our apartment complex to downtown each morning and back again each night. Dan and I had developed a good friendship over several months. Repeatedly he mentioned there was something different about me. I didn't need to get drunk like the other interns to have a good weekend. I had a more positive outlook on life than anyone he knew.

One night on the bus Dan noticed what I was reading. He said, "Oh, you're reading another Christian book."

"Dan, you know I'm a Christian," I answered, "but you don't know *why* I'm a Christian. Would you be interested in knowing why?"

"I would," Dan said. "Go ahead and tell me."

I thought, *Now? Here?!?* We were on a jam-packed but dead-silent bus. There had to be at least forty people, and they would hear every word. I gulped and then ventured into an explanation of how I had become a Christian, what following Jesus had done for my life, and the offer God makes to all of us through Jesus. It was nerve-wracking but exhilarating.

I was Bond. James Bond.

After college I went to a highly ranked law school and started hanging around some people who were smarter than my typical friends. In fact, they were smarter than me. When they discovered I was a Christian, they cross-examined my faith, trying to poke holes in everything I believed. Sometimes I didn't know what to say. Sometimes I was forced to do research and study harder than ever before. Occasionally, I felt stupid. Often I felt lonely. Always, I felt like a misunderstood minority. But each morning I woke up, praying for another chance to further our conversations. I watched my life closely, making sure I would provide no fodder for their opposition to Christianity. I relied on God to help me communicate in a way I never had before. And I loved every minute of it.

I was Bond. James Bond.

While in law school I decided to become a pastor and someday start a new church that might reach people like my friends back at college, the interns in DC, and my fellow students in law school. I transferred to seminary.

Suddenly, I was surrounded by Christians. I had no idea what to do with myself. I missed the sound of cursing so much I would play basketball with middle school kids at a court near my apartment complex just because their language and behavior was so bad. After seminary I did a ministry internship, followed by two years as an associate pastor at a church. During this entire time I hung out almost exclusively with Christian people. I also decided to stop listening to secular music and watching R-rated movies. I had confined my life to the interior of a Christian bubble. And one day I realized . . .

I was Bored. James Bored.

~⁓

It was about 1:00 in the morning when it happened. My wife was sleeping in the passenger seat next to me. We were moving to Virginia Beach to start a new church. I was listening to the radio, but for some reason I decided to listen to secular radio. A song came on that I had never heard called "Mr. Jones" by Counting Crows. The band's lead singer, Adam Duritz, sang, "Believe in me. Help me believe in anything. 'Cause I wanna be someone who believes . . ."

And I started thinking about this guy who wants to believe in something but can't. Who seems to have no faith, no hope, no real love. And he's writing songs begging for someone to talk to him and to give him something to believe in. Suddenly I started to feel ill. For several years I had been closing my eyes to people like Adam Duritz. I wouldn't even listen to their music because it might have a bad influence on me; but what influence did *not* listening to their music have on me? I had been learning about Jesus' mission and teaching others about it but not engaging in it myself. I had literally lost touch with non-Christian people. The Jesus life is about touching the sick and about being and sharing the good news with others. That was Jesus' mission for my life, but I had been ignoring it.

I was going to be sick. I was seriously about to throw up. I was driving 65 miles per hour down the highway and had no idea what to do. I rolled down my window and tried to project appropriately. That was when I learned that puke does not have much wind resistance. My vomit started to go out the window, thought better of it, reversed its course, and came right back at me. It flew right past my face, and all over my sleeping wife. She woke up and screamed, "What's happening to me?"

It was a horrible moment. But it was also a great moment. Because I realized my wife wasn't really the one asleep. *I was.* I had been sleepwalking through my Christian life the past four years. That vomit was meant for me. It was a holy wake-up call from God. And I made a commitment right then. I was going to live the Jesus life, not only touching the sick, but also fully engaging in *being* and *sharing* the good news. No longer would I be disappointed and bored with my Christian life.

A couple months later I was standing outside in front of a group of people about to tell them about Jesus. We had put flyers on the doors of about five thousand homes, inviting people to a picnic to hear about the new church starting in their community. We prayed for ten people. To our amazement, *104* showed up. I shared my testimony and the vision for a new church—a church for people who didn't like church. Everyone seemed interested, except this one guy. He was a big guy with huge forearms. He leaned against a tree as I spoke and his eyes were throwing daggers at me. Afterwards I started walking around, greeting everyone. I purposely avoided this dude, partly because I was temporarily without health insurance. Finally, I approached him and said, "Hey, my name is Vince."

"My name is Dave," he said, "and I *hate* church!"

He looked intense and his words were coated with venom. I thought, *I'm going to get beat up at my own picnic!* I started backing up slowly and asked, "Why do you hate church, Dave?"

Dave explained that he went to church as a child, but when his parents divorced, the church told his mother not to come back. Years later, when he and his wife had their first child they decided to give church another try. They walked in and sat down in a pew next to another family. The family looked Dave and his shoddily dressed family up and down and moved to a different pew. Dave finished his story, stared at me, and growled, "I really hate church!"

I wish that was the first, or last, time I heard something like that. But it's not. And it *kills* me.

The gospel is the most beautiful thing imaginable. There is a perfect Father who loves us so much he'll forgive everything; in fact, he loves us so much he was willing to have his Son lay down his life so that he could forgive everything. And not only does he offer forgiveness, he offers life in his kingdom. It's a life that begins here and now, a life that Jesus described as full and abundant.[2] A life the Bible says is characterized by love, joy, peace, patience, kindness, goodness, faithfulness, gentleness, and self-control.[3] A life that becomes dominated by that which is true, noble, right, pure, lovely, admirable, excellent, and praiseworthy.[4] Life in a kingdom where the poor are privileged, where those who mourn are comforted, where the meek are esteemed, where the hungry are filled, where the merciful receive mercy, the pure are rewarded, where peacemakers rule rather than peace-wreckers, and where the persecuted finally receive justice.[5] And life in this kingdom isn't *just* here and now; eventually it will be everywhere and everlasting. This gospel, the idea that there truly is that kind of a God, the sacrifice of his Son, the offer of forgiveness, the full and abundant life in the kingdom to be had here and there, now and forever—it's the most beautiful thing imaginable.

But somehow Christians have managed to make the good news sound like bad news. They've taken the luster off the gospel and made it something ugly.

This is what we have working against us. Jesus called us to be bearers of the gospel. We are to be the people known for living out his amazing grace. We are asked to take this precious idea, this beautiful life, and bring it wherever we go, holding it out for others to see, making it available to anyone interested. But instead Christians have become bearers of "gospel" tracts, featuring cartoon drawings of people in anguish as they smolder in hell. Christians have become known as those who are amazingly judgmental. The other night in my small group one lady said that her boss told her when they receive a check with a Scripture verse printed on it, nine times out of ten that check will bounce. Another guy who works for an insurance company told us their fraud department claims the first sign of fraud is when an answering machine message includes the words, "God bless you." Christians are despised by waitresses as those who leave the worst tips.

In a world where somehow Christians have made the good news sound like bad news and have given a black eye to the gospel, we need to understand what we're up against. There are a lot of Daves who are not interested in buying what we're selling.

So I looked Dave in the eye and said, "Dave, I don't blame you for hating church. And if I were you, I would probably never give church another chance. But it's not supposed to be that way. It *isn't* always that way. And our church *won't* be that way. I hope somehow you'll give us a chance. And Dave, listen, not everyone does it right, but life with God is really special. It's amazing. And I think it's what you want, what we all really want. Maybe it's not what you think it is . . . not what you've seen."

Dave gave me another death stare, grunted, and walked away.

The next week we started five small groups with the eighty-nine people from the picnic who had signed up for them. Dave's wife showed up for one of the groups. That night I said, "Hey everyone, tonight we're gonna just play games and get to know each other, but next week we'll start reading the Bible together. We're going to start with the book of John."

Dave's wife raised her hand and asked, "Why? Is that the first book of the Bible?"

A few weeks later Dave came with her. He was reeking of pot. His eyes were glazed over. I don't think he said a word the entire night. But he started showing up, at first occasionally and then more and more regularly. He came with us when we served homeless people. He watched as people's lives were changed. He listened as they encouraged and prayed for each other. Slowly he began engaging the Bible and the other people in the group. A year later, Dave gave his life to Jesus and was baptized. He couldn't help it. He had been exposed to the gospel that is truly beautiful, to the good news which really is good news, to life in the kingdom. How could he say no to that?

In fact, one hundred people accepted Jesus and were baptized the first year of our new church. Dave was baptized on the same night as a crack addict and a bisexual couple.

The Jesus life is all about touching the sick and "preaching" the gospel, the kingdom of God.[6] If we claim to love and follow Jesus and we're not living the life he lived, offers, and died for us to have, we *should* be disappointed and bored. Our disappointment and boredom is *good* because it's alerting us to the fact that something is wrong. It's like the "Check Engine" light on the dashboard. When it lights up, you don't ignore it; instead you realize something is wrong with the engine, and it needs to be examined. Well, actually, I do tend to ignore glowing lights on my dashboard. I know I shouldn't, but I'm just too busy to do anything about it. And eventually something in my car breaks down.

I've found the same to be true in my Christian life. I'm able to ignore the disappointment and boredom and often do, because I'm just too busy living life to realize that I'm not really living life. But then, eventually, God will do something to break *me* down and help me to face reality. Once it was a Counting Crows song on the radio and vomit all over my wife. Another time it was my son and a water park.

A few summers ago my wife and I and our then five-year-old son and two-year-old daughter went to Water Country USA, a big water park not far from where we live. They have a bunch of huge kiddie pools. Each has slides and all kinds of fun stuff. We played in one kiddie pool for a while. Then we walked about two hundred yards to the next one. My kids were repeatedly going down one big slide. My wife walked over to the other side of the pool where they had a big mushroom shower. Eventually my son, Dawson, asked, "Where's Mom?"

"She's over there by the mushroom water shower thing," I answered.

"Can I go get her?" he asked.

"Sure," I answered, "go ahead."

About five minutes later I grabbed my daughter and said, "Let's go get Mommy and Dawson."

So we went over to the shower. My wife, Jen, was still under it but all by herself.

I asked, "Where's Dawson?"

She said, "What are you talking about?"

"I sent him over about five minutes ago."

"I haven't seen him."

I started looking all over the kiddie pool. I didn't see him. I thought, *Don't freak out, Vince, he's here. Umm, blue bathing suit.* I looked for a blue bathing suit. No. *Uhh, light brown hair.* No. *He's in one of the slides.* No. I screamed, "Dawson?"

It had now been over ten minutes since we had seen our son. I continued to look. Soon it had been over fifteen minutes. I started *totally freaking out.* Like hyperventilating freaking out.

The kiddie pool was sort of in a valley. I ran up the hill to the sidewalk so I could have a better view of the whole pool. I looked down. He was not there. My heart started racing. My throat clenched up. My head was pounding. I looked again. He was not there. I wanted to *die.*

I looked up the sidewalk to my left. No. I looked down the sidewalk to my right. No. I looked in the pool again. No. It had been twenty minutes. I looked up the sidewalk to my left. And I saw the flash of a blue bathing suit amongst the hundreds of people. I squinted. Light brown hair. I called out, "Dawson? Dawson!"

The blue bathing suit with light brown hair was about fifty yards away from me. I yelled, "Dawson?"

Finally, the child in the blue bathing suit with light brown hair looked up, and it was my son. "Dawson!"

He saw me and his face went white. I ran towards him. He ran towards me and dove into my arms.

"Where were you?" I asked.

"I went to find Mommy," he said. "I thought she was at the pool we were at before."

I said, "You went all the way to the other pool by yourself?" I held him tight.

And suddenly I realized that what I had just experienced for a few brief moments must be somewhat like God's entire existence. The Bible says that we are God's dearly loved children. God loves us even more than we love our own kids. And Jesus said that those *without* God are his *lost* children. Can you imagine God's heart? If a parent feels as frantic as I did for my son when he was lost, can you imagine how great God's concern must be for his countless lost children wandering around without him? If a lost son causes me tremendous pain, can you imagine what God feels?

And I realized as I held my son that nothing can be as important as me helping God's other lost children back home and into his arms. And if I'm not doing that, I *should* be disappointed and bored.

So often we can ignore that. We can live life as Christians but basically avoid the Jesus life. And we act like it doesn't matter or like we can do other things to make up for it, but we can't.

Think about it this way: What if tomorrow you're eating a bowl of cereal when you notice a picture of a missing child on your milk carton. Your eyes explode. You know this kid! You know his parents! And you know where to find the kid! You realize that you can take action that will almost certainly return this child to his mother and father. But then you think, *Nah. I don't feel like doing that. But I do like that kid's parents. I think I'll start giving them 10 percent of my income. Oh, and I'll go over to their house every Sunday morning and do some chores for them. And I might even sing some songs to them while I'm there.*

Obviously, that's just insane. Every person would love to be given money, have someone serve them, and maybe even be serenaded. But if a parent has a kid who is missing, nothing else matters in comparison to getting that lost child home. And so if we could help make that happen, there's no way we wouldn't do it.

But how often do we give and serve and sing to God but ignore the fact that our heavenly Father has lost children whom we could help return to him? When we ignore that, what we're really ignoring is our Father's heart. We're ignoring the mission Jesus gave us. And we will be disappointed . . . and bored.

Jesus was clear about his mission: "The Son of Man came to seek and to save what was lost." "I have not come to call the righteous, but sinners." "Go and make disciples." "Go into all the world and preach the good news to all creation." "You will be my witnesses."[7] We *must* engage in the mission Jesus has for us.

The only issue is *how*. Christians have an image problem. The good news we offer has gotten a bad reputation. And so a big part of the *how* is that we need to make the gospel beautiful again. We must remove the trappings that have accumulated over time from tradition and culture so people can experience the natural beauty of God's good news for them. We need to show people what life in the kingdom is like before we invite them into it.

When I first became a Christian and started telling people about my new discovery, I had very little results. Most people didn't get angry, they just didn't care. They had no interest in the God I had become so passionate about or in life in his kingdom. I couldn't understand why. Until finally I realized: it was because there was very little integrity to my gospel. People didn't view the good news I was sharing with them *as* good news. At best they had no real experience with Jesus. But most of them had actually been turned off by Christians in the past.

I finally started to see them become interested in what I was saying, and even respond to it, when I had time to build relationships with them. When they had time to inspect my new life. When I had the opportunity to serve them, to display the joy God had brought into my life. When they were able to see the gospel as actually being beautiful, then they could hear the good news as actually being good news.

And I've found that usually it takes awhile to accomplish this, although sometimes it can happen surprisingly fast.

Staff members at my church take one day each month to fast and pray. It's a day designed to get away and get close to God, to focus on him and pray for the church. I decided to spend one prayer and fasting day at Burger King. I know that sounds bizarre, but I wasn't going to eat. Normally, I go to a park or the beach on my prayer day, but it was cold outside, so I wanted a place where I could be inside but by myself. When I do my fasting day I don't eat, but I do drink, so I thought, *I'll go to Burger King, get a Coke, sit there for a couple hours, read my Bible, and write in my journal.* So I went in, got my Coke, sat down, and started reading.

Two minutes later a dirty, smelly guy came walking up. He was obviously extremely poor, probably homeless. He started pacing in front of my table. I glanced up several times but tried not to make eye contact because I wanted to keep reading my Bible. After all, this was a day for me. My goal was to get me closer to God. Finally, I felt guilty and thought, *This isn't right. Vince, you need to take some time, die to yourself, and love this guy.* So I asked, "Hey, can I help you with anything?"

Turns out this guy was from India. He started talking, but I could barely decipher his words. Finally, he handed me a piece of paper. It was a job application for Burger King. I said, "Oh, you want to apply here. Do you need help filling this out?" He nodded yes, so we got to work. It was difficult. One question asked about experience. I think he said he used to be a cook. In Florida? India? Indiana? Another requested his home address, but he didn't have one. It took nearly an hour. Finally, we were done and he walked to the counter to turn it in. I thought, *It's good that I helped him, but I'm glad that's over.* I went back to reading.

One minute later he was sitting back at my table. I said, "Oh. Hi." He sat and stared at me. I thought, *Maybe he's hungry.* "Do you need something to eat?" I asked.

He said yes, so I gave him a few dollars. And he appreciated it. He really appreciated it. He grabbed both my hands and started rubbing them all over his face and neck. I thought, *Oh . . . my . . . goodness! This is so weird!* Finally, after the thirty most awkward seconds of my life, he grabbed my money and disappeared. I thought, *Wow. Well, it's good that I helped him. But I am so glad that's over.* I went back to reading.

Two minutes later he was sitting back at my table. This time he had a burger and fries. I thought, *Maybe he just needs someone to talk to.* I started a conversation, and then he asked me about the Bible I was reading. I started to explain that I believed in Jesus. A smile erupted on his face and he pulled his wallet out. He proudly showed me a picture of Jesus. I said, "Yeah, that's who I'm telling you about!" Then he proceeded to show me pictures of Buddha, Muhammad, a goat, Reggie Jackson, there may have been some of Regis Philbin, the Dali Lama, and Bea Arthur in there as well. He then became very serious and asked, "Do you know what God's name is?"

I said, "Yes, I'm trying to explain to you—I believe his name is Jesus. Jesus is God's Son."

He said, "No! God's name is Twenty-one."

"Huh?"

"God's name is Twenty-one. Do you understand?" he demanded.

I said, "Yeah, you think God's name is Twenty-one."

He insisted, "Nooo! God's name is Twenty-one. You understand?"

"Yeah, you just said God's name is Twenty-one."

His voice was rising, "No. No! God's name is Twenty-one."

I repeated, "God's name is Twenty-one."

"No! God's name is Twenty-one!"

"Got it. God's name is Twenty-one."

"No! God's name is Twenty-one!"

Finally, I put an end to our Abbot and Costello routine and asked him to please explain what he meant. He tried. I think what he was struggling to say was that he believed that all religions worship the same God and that God is called by twenty-one different names in the various religions of the world, and so he has twenty-one names.

"Okay, I understand now," I said. "But I believe there is only one God, and Jesus was his Son."

He asked, "Do you know who God is today?"

I answered, "Twenty-one?"

"No," he said. "Today, you are God to me."

"No, I'm not God," I responded.

"Yes, you are," he countered.

"No," I explained. "I'm trying to show you the love of God, but I'm not God."

"No. Today you love me," he said. "You help me. You feed me. Who is God? He loves, he helps, he feeds. Today, you are God to me."

In one sense he was theologically wrong, because I'm certainly not God. But in another sense, he was right. Because God *has* asked me to represent him, to be his ambassador.[8]

We need to *be* the good news before we share the good news so that our gospel has integrity. We need to make the gospel beautiful again. We need to lose all the trappings so people can experience the natural beauty of God's good news. We need to show people what life in God's kingdom is like before we invite them into it.

There are times when I don't feel capable of doing that well, but I've learned that I can. If I am really living life with Jesus, then I am fully capable of living the Jesus life, because really, it's not me living it—Jesus is living it through me.

Four years into our church we experienced our first death. One of the core couples in our church lost their teenage daughter in a car accident the night before Easter. I had to announce it, and after I did, our Easter service became more of a funeral service. The next morning the girl's father woke up early and was unable to go back to sleep. He walked down to his living room around 5:30 a.m. He grabbed his Bible and sat on the couch. As he did, he noticed something through the window. There was something in his backyard. In the darkness it looked like a large lump on the ground. He squinted and realized it was a person. Eventually he realized it was Dave, the guy I thought was going to beat me up at the picnic. Dave was on his knees praying for the family. Who knows how or when Dave had arrived or how long he had been there. But he stayed for quite a while, praying for this family.

He had turned into a secret agent.

And he was definitely not bored.

PART 4

REGRESS

WHEN YOU'RE WEARING THE OLD T-SHIRT

QUESTIONS 16

So here's the question I'm learning to ask: if I'm disappointed, *why* am I disappointed?

⌒

I became a Christian in the summer of 1990. That same week my father bought me a car. I was twenty years old and had already owned four cars. I think the most I had paid for any of them was five hundred dollars. Each looked like it had lost in a demolition derby. One was a LeCar. I don't think they make LeCars anymore, but just in case you are thinking of buying one, let me warn you: they are LeCrap. Another was a Mustang. That may sound tough, but this car was anything but. The entire front right quarter panel was covered in duct tape. After owning the car for a few weeks, I wondered how bad the metal was under the duct tape. So I methodically removed each strip, finally revealing . . . nothing. There was *nothing* under the duct tape. Seriously. The duct tape had been stuck to the two closest pieces of remaining metal and pulled tight across the chasm. I realized that I had bought three-quarters of a car. I was upset until I realized that at three hundred dollars, I had still paid only a hundred bucks per quarter.

But the car my father bought me the week I became a Christian was sweet. It was a 1988 Nissan Maxima, only two years old and with a mere fifteen thousand miles on it. It cost $8,500, seventeen times the most I had ever laid down! It gleamed silver and I don't mean duct tape silver, but shiny glinting silver that made heads turn. All the metal was present and accounted for. It had leather seats, plus electronic keypad locks on the doors. And this car *talked*. It was programmed to say things like "Your door is ajar" and "Please buckle your seatbelt" and "Vince, you are sooo hot." Okay, it never said that, but I imagined it, because my car talked with a smokin' girl's voice. My friends were scheduling dates with my car. I considered starting a 1-900 sex line with my car but wasn't sure how much guys would pay to hear "Your left front tire is low on air."

I was strutting around like Burt Reynolds circa 1978 (*with* the moustache), like Tom Selleck circa 1984 (*with* the moustache), like Tom Cruise circa 1991 (*without* the wacko Scientology stuff and the jumping on Oprah's couch bit), like George Clooney circa 1997 (without the nipple-popping Batsuit). (Okay, maybe *with* the nipple-popping Batsuit.) You get the idea. My life rocked. I had become a Christian *and* I went from driving a rolling heap of cow dung to cruising around in my almost brand-new, female companion of a Nissan Maxima.

One month later my car was gone.

I was making a left turn off of Main Street in Buffalo, New York, when some dude's car assaulted mine like a lion on a gimpy gazelle. I woke up in the hospital. I was very confused. My body felt like it had been through a food processor. They told me my head split open like a cantaloupe, the gash just above my eyes required twenty-four stitches. Bandages circled my head.

I also learned that my car was totaled. "What?" I screamed. "Did you at least save the voice box? . . . No. Nooo! . . . She . . . she . . . she never even said goodbye."

I went the next several weeks looking like a mummy from my eyebrows up and without a car. Finally, my mother kindly offered to buy me a new one. I breathed a huge sigh of relief and said, "Thanks, Mom." She smiled, "Sure, honey," and handed me . . . three hundred dollars.

This was only a few months after I became a Christian, and I was *severely* disappointed with my life. I could not believe this happened to me. I lived twenty years *without* God but never suffered a major injury, never had any of my cars totaled, never walked around looking like I wandered off a horror movie set. Now, *after* giving my life to God, all of this had happened. For a while I felt like the rug had been pulled out from under me. Hadn't Jesus promised real, full, abundant life? Was *this* it? Wasn't God a heavenly father who was supposed to take care of me? Is *this* the best he could do?

So, *why* was I disappointed? Was it because I wasn't really living life with Jesus? No, that wasn't it. My faith was new and exciting, I was passionate about God, I was growing in intimacy with him every day. I was still a rookie at it all, but as best I knew how I was going into the tent of meeting to have face time with God every morning and being monklike the rest of my day.

Was it because I wasn't really living the Jesus life? No, it wasn't that either. I was looking for opportunities to touch people with God's love. I was being and sharing the good news about Jesus and his kingdom with people whenever I had the chance.

So, why was I disappointed? I was experiencing the reality that even life with Jesus has some boring and bad parts. I was mired in problems that even authentic Christ followers have to go through, but I was unprepared for it. I went into the Christian life with unrealistic expectations, and my reality wasn't matching what I thought I would experience.

It wasn't long before my disappointment dissipated. And as I look back on my difficult time I realize that even though I struggled with disappointment, still I handled what happened in a very different way than I would have previously. I wasn't happy with what I went through, but I was okay with it. I possessed a peace I never had before. I *was* living life with Jesus and living the Jesus life.

⌒

I mentioned earlier how when my wife was pregnant for the second time she had all kinds of problems with her pregnancy. She was throwing up repeatedly. Soon she was admitted into the hospital for a week. She returned home connected to an IV pump she had to carry around in a backpack. A nurse informed me that I would be in charge of changing the IV line, which entered in through her arm and pumped a thick, milky-white substance straight into her heart.

Soon the IV line became infected. The doctor assured me it was nothing I had done. He told me he was re-admitting my wife into the hospital.

During this time my son was a year and a half old and my church was two and a half years old. Both led me to deal with a lot of crap. Unfortunately, my church did not wear a diaper. With my wife out of commission, my life became insane. I had new business cards printed up:

Vince Antonucci

- Full-Time Husband
- Upchuck Cleaner-Upper
- Full-Time (and Basically Single) Dad
- Full-Time Pastor
- Part-Time Nurse
- Someone please shoot me

During this time I once again was *severely* disappointed with my life.

But *why* was I disappointed?

I wasn't living life with Jesus, and because of that I wasn't really living the Jesus life. This was when my friend Kevin came over and challenged me to spend time with God, which ended up turning things around for me. Now looking back, I realize that the complications of my wife's illness and the madness of my schedule at the time only accentuated a problem that had already crept into my life. My faith had become stale and crusty; I was increasingly indifferent about God. I was mostly looking out for me. I still believed. I still behaved correctly. But I wasn't living life with Jesus. Jesus continued to call me on vacation with him, but for a while I stayed home and ignored his invitation. I was just wearing the T-shirt. I was Emily.

The question I'm learning to ask is, if I'm disappointed, *why* am I disappointed?

Maybe you need to ask yourself that question too.

Are you dealing with the reality that even life with Jesus can be rough at times? Or are you not really living in the presence of Jesus, let alone being his presence in the lives of others?

Perhaps there's something you're not doing. It might be something you used to do but stopped. Or it could be something you've never done, and the reality is that you've never truly experienced the life Jesus has for you. Take a long hard look at your life. Is it marked by expectancy, by a journey out of routine and into adventure, by a deep sense of relaxing? If not, or if they are exceptions more than the rule, is it possible that there's something about the Jesus life you're missing?

Here are some other questions I'm learning to ask myself:

If I feel most alive when I'm watching a movie or playing a video game or reading a book or watching sports, if those are consistently the best parts of my day, what does that say about my life? Shouldn't it be more exciting to live *my* life than to watch someone else live *theirs*?

In the Bible Jesus led his followers into dangerous places. Do I often find myself in dangerous places? And if not, what does that mean?

Despite being completely righteous, Jesus attracted the worst of sinners. Are sinful people drawn to me, or are they put off by my so-called righteousness?

When Jesus came into contact with people, their lives were radically transformed. Are people's lives changed by knowing me?

Do I have sinful habits I can't seem to shake? Why?

What do I dream about? What does my mind automatically turn to? What should it?

Would the people who know me best say my life is characterized by love, joy, peace, patience, kindness, goodness, faithfulness, gentleness, and self-control?

Do I read the Bible and pray because I can't wait to spend time with God or because it's what I'm supposed to do as a Christian?

And why do I skip my Bible and prayer time on weekends or when I'm out of town? Is that time really just a habit, a part of my routine, or is it the sacred conversation it's supposed to be?

Am I living in a safe Christian bubble? If so, why does the world scare me?

What do I use to escape from my problems? Why do I need to escape from my problems at all? Shouldn't Jesus help me handle them?

Do I serve because I get to or because I have to?

Do I get upset about things in a way that is disproportionate to their importance?

What are the top items on my current wish list?

The word *Christian* literally means "little Christ"—so am I a Christian or do I just call myself one?

Why isn't Jesus enough for me?

Maybe these questions will be helpful for you too. And maybe, for each of us, the answers will be revealing.

Sometimes I discover that I'm disappointed because life can be disappointing. Life can be really difficult, and no one gets excited about having to deal with that.

But sometimes I have to face the fact that I'm not living life with Jesus, or I'm not living the Jesus life. Perhaps you'll have to face the same hard truth.

WHISPER

17

But what if you've asked the questions, you've done a serious evaluation of your life, and you come to the conclusion that you *are* living life with Jesus, and you *are* living the Jesus life . . . but you're still disappointed? Why? What then?

Perhaps you're facing the reality that life (this side of heaven) stinks sometimes. There are promises in the Bible about heaven—like how God will wipe away every tear from our eyes—but we don't get those promises about life here and now.[1] Instead, Jesus promises, "In this world you will have trouble."[2] Jesus tells us he came to bring us full life, but it's not a problem-free life.

I think one of the most interesting people in the Bible is Elijah. Elijah's story in 1 Kings 17–19 is fascinating because he experienced so many phenomenal highs and so many drastic lows. His was perhaps the most roller-coaster-like life of anyone in the Bible.

For instance, God chose Elijah to be his prophet. This was a big deal—it was like winning American Idol. God would speak directly to his prophets, and his prophets spoke directly to the people for God. It was the highest honor, totally prestigious. And the first ministry assignment we see Elijah carry out is to go and confront the evil King Ahab. He went in and confronted the most powerful man in the nation. Imagine the adrenaline rush.

So Elijah prophesies and informs Ahab that there would be no dew or rain in the next few years unless Elijah says so. Then God immediately says to Elijah, "Run!" And so Elijah hightails it to a place called Kerith Brook. And this has to be an incredible *low*. He's all alone, hiding for his life; he has no cell phone coverage.

It doesn't seem like he'll last long out there. There's nothing to eat, and a drought has hit that will soon dry up the brook Elijah is relying on for water. But God promises Elijah he'll take care of him. And he does. God sends ravens to Elijah each day with food and even meat for him to eat. And God miraculously keeps the brook from drying up so Elijah has water. And so, even in this low time, Elijah has a real *high* as he experiences the provision of God.

But then the brook dries up. Where there was once water, there's now nothing but sand and rocks. And Elijah hits another *low*. What does this say about God? Is he incapable of extending the miracle? Has he stopped caring?

Then God speaks to Elijah again, and tells him to go to a town called Zarephath where a widow will take care of him. Zarephath is nearly 100 miles away, so Elijah now has a long walk ahead of him in the middle of a drought. Zarephath is also the birthplace of Baal worship, which is what Elijah has been taking a stand against. He is about to go into the heart of darkness. And in the culture of the day, widows could hardly be any lower on the social totem pole. They fell somewhere

just above slaves and just below vomitorium scrubbers.*
But Elijah would have to rely on a widow. A new *low*.

When Elijah arrives in Zarephath he meets the widow,
who is preparing a last meal for herself and her son,
because they have run out of food and are about to die.
Elijah asks for that last meal for himself and promises
that God will provide for her. And that's exactly what happens. Miraculously God provides a continual supply of
flour and oil. Elijah stays in the guestroom of the house,
enjoying fresh bread every day. This is a real *high*.

But then things take a huge turn for the worse. Out
of nowhere the widow's son gets sick and dies. The
widow totally blames Elijah. This is probably a record
low. Imagine being taken in by a family and then being
blamed for the death of the son of that family. But then,
in a moment of extraordinary boldness, Elijah says to the
lady, "Give me your son." And with great faith he prays
that God will raise her boy from the dead . . . and God
does it! This is the first time in the Bible that a person
is raised from the dead. As far as we know, it had never
happened in the history of the world, and Elijah is the
one God uses to pull it off. Talk about a *high*.

Later, Elijah confronts King Ahab again and challenges him and hundreds of prophets of the false gods
to a steel cage match. It would be a contest that would
determine once and for all the identity of the *true* God.
The king gladly agrees, everyone shows up to watch, and
Elijah wins a decisive victory making it indisputable that
he has been in the right. This is probably the greatest
high of Elijah's life.

*Earlier in this book I mentioned that foot washers were the bottom
of the totem pole, just below elephant proctologists. So, if you're keeping
track, the order from the bottom of the totem pole is foot washers, elephant
proctologists, vomitorium scrubbers, widows, slaves. If you're curious, the
next two spots are taken by professional back shavers and priests assigned to
nudist colonies. In more modern times, bulletproof underwear testers have
worked their way onto that list.

And immediately after, Elijah again finds himself running for his life until he collapses under a broom tree in the desert, praying to die. Exhausted, he falls asleep. Finally, after being served some "angel food cake," taking another nap, and eating again, the worn-out prophet is revitalized only to travel forty days and forty nights so he can go up a mountain to hide from his enemies in a cave.

In all of his lows, Elijah felt extreme disappointment. He didn't whistle his way through it, he didn't turn his frown upside down, he didn't have the joy of the Lord. He was *down*. After winning the cage match and just before running up the mountain to hide, we find Elijah wanting to die. He is begging God, not for joy but for death.

I can relate to Elijah's story. Sometimes the problem is me. Sometimes I'm not living life with Jesus or living the Jesus life, or whatever, and I know it's *my* fault that I'm disappointed with how things are going.

But sometimes the problem *isn't* me. It's life. My life goes up and down like John Travolta's career, and I love the highs but am completely bewildered by the lows. And I ask God to explain to me why I have to go through the crud I go through, but I almost never get an answer. *So what do we do when we're feeling that way?*

What I've been learning is that sometimes we don't really need answers; we just need *the Answer*. Sometimes maybe even the right explanations wouldn't satisfy us like we believe they would, and we need to realize that the only thing that will truly satisfy us is God himself.

I've shared some about my wife's difficult pregnancies, but not the problems we experienced postdelivery. The day after my son Dawson was born he had a high temperature and was dehydrated. The doctors feared meningitis and later a heart complication. For seven days we remained in the hospital as they watched him closely and ran a battery of tests.

On one of those days, the doctor told us he was going to perform a spinal tap on my son. We objected, but he explained that it was necessary to find out what was wrong. He explained that a long needle would be injected into our baby's back and that it would be a little painful, but the discomfort wouldn't last long. I said I would come and watch. He told me not to. I wouldn't want to see what was going to happen. I explained that there was no way I would leave my son alone.

So I watched. And it was *awful* to see that happen to my son. I cringed. I cried. But I also knew it was necessary.

As soon as the operation was over, my son was handed to me and I held him. He was crying and looking at me with big, confused eyes. And I could have given him answers. I could have explained that he was dehydrated, that his heart rate seemed slightly irregular, that the procedure he just went through would eliminate some of the possible problems and maybe even reveal the cause of his symptoms. But I knew he wouldn't understand. And though something inside of him probably wanted answers and an explanation, instead I just held him and whispered softly to him.

When Elijah was up on the mountain, he wanted answers. He wanted an explanation. And God could easily have enlightened Elijah, sharing with him why he had to go through those lows.

I mean, even I can look at the life of Elijah and see some of what might have been the logic behind what he had gone through. Even I could give some answers to Elijah.

For example, Elijah, isn't it possible that God whisked you away from the high of confronting King Ahab and all the fame you would have received from that because God loves you so much he didn't want you to derive your significance from what other people think of you or from your accomplishments? Maybe God took you to Kerith Brook so you could have some one-on-one intimacy with him?

And, Elijah, couldn't it be that God allowed the brook to dry up because he didn't want you to put your faith in ravens and streams? And did you really want to stay there forever? Did you want being all alone at Kerith Brook to be the end of your story? Didn't God have to do something to move you on from there?

And Elijah, after spending time in that safe haven, couldn't it be that God told you to go to Zarephath so you would learn that God's love and provision doesn't depend on being in a safe place, that you could be just as secure with God in a very dangerous place?

Elijah, couldn't it be that God allowed the widow's son to die because he wanted you to understand that nothing was impossible with him? Maybe he wanted to prepare you for the tough challenges that lay ahead by showing you that no obstacle is too big for God's power?

Elijah was up on the mountain, and he wanted explanations for all the lows he had gone through. And I'm not God, but even I can figure out some of the possible reasons. But God did not give Elijah any explanations. Instead he gave Elijah *himself*. God showed up and spoke to Elijah in a gentle whisper.[3]

I've been in Elijah's situation. I've never hid on a mountain, and since I've become a Christian I haven't wanted to die, but I have felt extreme disappointment.

One time I was in New Mexico at a pastor conference, and I had a very unsettled feeling about things. Our church seemed to be doing great at the time, but for some reason I had this sense that what I was doing for God wasn't sufficient. One night the conference offered an extended prayer time. I sat in this huge sanctuary and felt distraught. I thought back to the bizarre circumstances through which I had become a Christian and how, since no one had helped me, it was almost like God reached down and made sure I would know him. And I prayed, *Why God? Is there some big thing you want me to do with my life? Am I doing it? Am I missing it? What great thing do you have for me? Why did you reach down and save me?*

And God showed up. I heard a voice. Not out loud. No one else heard it. It was just a whisper, deep in my heart. And the words I heard were completely unexpected. God whispered to me:

You are enough.

It was as if God was telling me, "Vince, I love you. I saved you because I wanted you. You are enough. It's not about what you do for me."

Another time, years later, I was feeling distressed again. This time things at the church were not going so great. And I had this sense that what God was doing for me wasn't sufficient. I continued to sink lower and lower, growing increasingly anxious. Finally, one morning, I let God have it. I prayed, *Why, God? Isn't there something bigger you can do with my life than this? I mean, I work my butt off for you, and the results I should be seeing just aren't there. You said you would build your church. You're supposed to care about this more than I do. So why aren't you acting? Why aren't you doing something? Even if you won't do it for yourself, which you should, would you at least do it for me? Because I am sick of pouring myself into this and not seeing a lot of results. And I am really tired of having no joy about it.*

And God showed up. Again, I heard a voice. Like the last time, it wasn't out loud. God whispered to me,

I am enough.

It was like God was saying, "Vince, I'll decide what kind of results your church will or won't have, but either way you can't get your joy from that. Whether you're content or not can't depend on your circumstances. I am enough for you, Vince. And if you can't learn and live in that, then nothing will ever be enough for you."

Both of these times I wanted explanations. But God didn't give me answers, he gave me himself. He showed up and whispered softly to me.

The week after my son was born, as the doctors conducted test after test, we waited for result after result. I hated every moment of it and was in constant despair. I was losing it. I felt helpless. Finally, they gave him a clean bill of health and sent us home. That was a Tuesday afternoon. Wednesday afternoon my wife was lying on our couch with a high temperature, freezing with chills, and shaking uncontrollably. Thursday morning she was admitted back into the hospital with a mysterious uterus infection and a 104.7 temperature. She and Dawson spent the next five days back in the hospital together. Jen kept getting worse. They couldn't figure out what was wrong. I flew right back into freak-out mode.

One night Jen's temperature had gone back up over 104. She was shaking so bad it was like she was vibrating. The nurse tore in and immediately tried to get her temperature down. I stared at the scene in front of me. *This is unbelievable,* I thought. *I can't take this anymore. I am so alone.*

Finally, Jen's temperature came down a little, and the nurse left. Jen turned to me and said, "I know I'm going to be okay."

"Why?" I asked. "How can you know that?"

She answered, "Because while all that was happening I was singing a song to God, and he just kind of let me know he's here, and he loves us."

I asked what she was singing.

And she sang, still shaking, "Hold me Jesus, 'cause I'm shaking like a leaf. You have been my King of glory; won't you be my Prince of peace?"[4]

The difference between my wife and me was that she was listening for the whisper, and I wasn't.

~~~

I believe the ideas in this book are at the core of Christianity and of life. Being a Christian is about living life with Jesus—really abiding in him. And it's about living the Jesus life—really abounding in him.

But even closer to the core are the facts that I am enough for God, and God is enough for me.

I hope the ideas in this book find their way deep within you and come out as you journey through life.

But even more, I hope you know and remember this:

You are enough for God.
And God is enough for you.

And when you forget, listen for the whisper.

ACKNOWLEDGMENTS

I'm supposed to "acknowledge" the people I appreciate. I think "acknowledging" is kind of an odd term for it. It sounds like I'm recognizing the fact that they exist, but they don't need that. They exist without my acknowledging it. A better title would be "Appreciatements." But, unfortunately, that's not even a word, so I am forced to acknowledge. Here goes . . .

Thank you, God, for giving me a story to tell; Jesus, for inviting me to live life with authentic passion; and Holy Spirit, for guiding me through this adventure.

Thank you to Jen, Dawson, and Marissa—if every family in the world were lined up, I would choose you. I can't imagine this journey without you.

Thank you to Baker Books and especially my editor and friend Chad Allen. Chad, this book exists only because of your belief in me. I totally appreciate everything you've put into improving this book.

Thank you to John Burke for helping to make this book happen.

Thank you to my church, Forefront, and especially our staff. Without all of you I would never be asked to write a book or have anything worthwhile to say in it. You are an amazing church, and I'm honored to be a part.

Thank you to the people who read this book along the way and gave me feedback: Jen, Juli, Jen, James, Joe, Tim, and I'm probably forgetting someone.

I acknowledge that all of you exist, and offer you my appreciatements.

NOTES

Chapter 2 Emily

1. See John 10:10.

Chapter 3 Alive

1. John 10:10 (paraphrased).
2. Irenaeus, *Against Heresies*, bk. 4, chap. 20, para. 7, quoted in *The Early Christian Fathers: A Selection from the Writings of the Fathers from St. Clement of Rome to St. Athanasius*, ed. Henry Bettenson (Oxford: Oxford University Press, 1956), 76.
3. Matthew 11:28.

Chapter 4 Abide

1. John 15:4–5 NASB (emphasis added).

Chapter 6 Hungry

1. John 6:27.
2. John 6:35.
3. John 6:53 (paraphrased).
4. John 6:54.
5. John 6:55.
6. John 6:56.
7. The disciples apparently had access to a portal into the future where they spent their time listening to Steven Wright do stand-up, or perhaps stealing his jokes from Internet sources like "Steven Wright Quotes," BrainyQuote, http://www.brainyquote.com/quotes/authors/s/steven_wright.html.

Chapter 7 Follow

1. Eugene H. Peterson, *A Long Obedience in the Same Direction: Discipleship in an Instant Society* (Downers Grove, IL: InterVarsity, 1980).
2. John 13:37; 11:16 (both paraphrased).
3. See Genesis 1:2.
4. John 4:1–42; Luke 19:1–10; and John 5:1–14.

Chapter 8 Glow

1. 2 Corinthians 3:13 (emphasis added); see Exodus 34:29–35. The surrounding story is found in the book of Exodus.
2. Jeremiah 10:5 portrays the absurdity of a "god" who cannot talk: "Like a scarecrow in a melon patch, their idols cannot speak; they must be carried because they cannot walk."
3. Augustine quoted in Richard Foster, *Prayer: Finding the Heart's True Home* (New York: HarperCollins, 1992), 255.
4. Brennan Manning, *Abba's Child* (Colorado Springs: NavPress, 1994), 126–28.
5. Foster, *Prayer*, 3–4.
6. Zephaniah 3:17 gives us this picture of God's heart for us: "The LORD your God is with you, he is mighty to save. He will take great delight in you, he will quiet you with his love, he will rejoice over you with singing."

Chapter 9 Monk

1. John 15:4 NASB; Matthew 28:20 NIV.
2. 1 Thessalonians 5:16–18.
3. Brother Lawrence wrote: "The most holy practice . . . the most essential for the spiritual life, is the practice of the presence of God . . . to find joy in his divine company . . . speaking humbly and conversing lovingly with him at all times, every moment." Brother Lawrence, *The Practice of the Presence of God* (Hodder & Stoughton, 1985), http://www.wcr.ab.ca/news/2005/0221/prayer022105.shtml. And, "an habitual, silent, and secret conversation of the soul with God, which often causes me joys and raptures inwardly, and sometimes also outwardly, so great that I am forced to use means to moderate them and prevent their appearance to others." Brother Lawrence, *The Practice of the Presence of God* (Uhrichsville: Barbour & Company, 1993), 37–38.
4. Thomas Merton, *The Wisdom of the Desert* (New York: New Directions Publishing, 1960), 3.
5. Henri Nouwen, *The Way of the Heart* (New York: Harper Collins, 1991), 69. See 1 Thessalonians 5:17.
6. Theophan the Recluse quoted in Timothy Ware, ed., *The Art of Prayer: An Orthodox Anthology* (London: Faber & Faber, 1966), 110.
7. Macarius the Great quoted in Irenee Hasherr, *The Name of Jesus*, trans. Charles Cummings (Kalamazoo, MI: Cistercian, 1978), 314.
8. Martin Luther, a former monk himself, allegedly once said, "For when one flees and becomes a monk, it sounds as though he were saying, 'Pfui!

How the people stink! How damnable is their state! I will be saved, and let them go to the devil!' If Christ had fled thus and become such a holy monk, who would have died for us or rendered satisfaction for us poor sinners? Would it be the monks, with their strict lives of flight?"

9. Philip Yancey, *Prayer* (Grand Rapids: Zondervan, 2006), 51.

10. Ibid.

11. The idea we get from the Bible is that God is one essence (one *what*) and three persons (three *who*s): the Father, the Son (incarnate as Jesus of Nazareth), and the Holy Spirit. In Christianity, this idea as a doctrine or teaching about God (called the Trinity) has long been expressed as "three persons in one God." Yet even the world's greatest theologians can't fully explain this mystery. But in terms of *perichoresis*, some have used this Greek word to describe the Father, Jesus, and the Holy Spirit indwelling one another and living together in community in a way that is so close, so tight, and so intertwined that though three, they somehow are one. The interplay is like a dance. See John 14–17.

12. This would be what Jesus was referring to in John 14:20 when he said, "I am in my Father, and you [are] in me, and I [am] in you," and what he meant in John 15:4 when he said, "Abide in me, and I [will abide] in you" (NASB).

13. Yancey, *Prayer*, 181.

14. The Jesus Prayer quoted in Nouwen, *Way of the Heart*, 85–86.

15. Anne Lamott, *Traveling Mercies* (New York: Pantheon, 1999), 82.

Chapter 10 Abound

1. Romans 8:29 TLB.

2. John 14:12 (emphasis added).

3. 1 Corinthians 15:58 NASB (emphasis added).

4. See, for example, F. Hauck, "*perisseúō*," *Theological Dictionary of the New Testament, Abridged in One Volume*, ed. Gerhard Kittel and Gerhard Friedrich, trans. Geoffrey W. Bromiley (Grand Rapids: Eerdmans, 1985), 864.

5. 2 Peter 1:3.

6. 2 Peter 1:4 (emphasis added).

7. This idea that God enables a Christian to take part in his own nature is taught throughout the New Testament. In Acts 2:38 it's called receiving the Holy Spirit. In Ephesians 3:19 it's described as being filled with God. In Galatians 2:20 it's expressed as Jesus living in us.

8. John 15:4–5 NASB (emphasis added).

Chapter 11 Speed

1. See Luke 10:27.

2. Luke 10:28.

3. Kosuke Koyama, *Three Mile an Hour God* (Maryknoll, NY: Orbis Books, 1980), chap. 1, quoted in Tony Lane, *The Lion Concise Book of Christian Thought* (Oxford: Lion Hudson, 1984), 225–26.

4. In fact, of the Ten Commandments, one of the *most* discussed, commented on, and reinforced commandment in the Old Testament is God's directive to keep or observe the Sabbath. Repeatedly, God reminds his people he wants them to take a day of rest.

5. Matthew 11:28–30 Message.

6. James Swanson, "נֶפֶשׁ [*nafash*]," *A Dictionary of Biblical Languages with Semantic Domains: Hebrew (Old Testament)*, (Oak Harbor, WA: Logos Research Systems, Inc., 1997), [Online] Available: Logos Library System. "Six days do your work, but on the seventh day do not work, so that your ox and your donkey may rest and the slave born in your household, and the alien as well, *may be refreshed* [*vyinafesh*]" (Exod. 23:12, emphasis added); see also Exodus 31:17 where this same word is used to say that God *rested* or *was refreshed* after his work of creating the world.

Chapter 12 Naked

1. Genesis 2:25 ESV.
2. See Genesis 3.
3. C. S. Lewis, *The Four Loves* (New York: Harcourt, 1988), 121.

Chapter 13 Die

1. Mark 8:34–35.
2. John 13:14–17.

Chapter 14 Touch

1. Mark 1:40.
2. Leviticus 13:45.
3. Mark 1:40.
4. Mark 1:41–42.
5. See Luke 7:22–23 (paraphrased).
6. Check out Matthew 10:1, 5–8; Mark 3:13–15; Luke 9:1–6.
7. See David Van Biema, "Mother Teresa's Crisis of Faith," *Time*, August 23, 2007, http://www.time.com/time/world/article/0,8599,1655415-1,00.html.
8. Malcolm Muggeridge, *Something Beautiful for God* (1971; repr., New York: Harper & Row, 1986), 49 (emphasis added).
9. Mother Teresa, *My Life for the Poor*, ed. José Luis González-Balado and Janet N. Playfoot (New York: Ballentine Books, 1985), 60.
10. Edward W. Desmond, "A Pencil in the Hand of God," *Time*, December 4, 1989, http://www.time.com/time/reports/motherteresa/t891204.html.

Chapter 15 Mission

1. See Matthew 28:18–20; Mark 16:15; Acts 1:8.
2. See John 10:10.
3. See Galatians 5:22–23.
4. See Philippians 4:8.

5. See Matthew 5:3–10.

6. See Luke 9:2, 6.

7. See Luke 19:10; Matthew 9:13; 28:19–20; Mark 16:15; Acts 1:8.

8. See 2 Corinthians 5:20.

Chapter 17 Whisper

1. See Revelation 21:4.

2. John 16:33; see 1 Corinthians 7:28.

3. See 1 Kings 19:12.

4. Rich Mullins, "Hold Me Jesus," *A Liturgy, a Legacy & a Ragamuffin Band*, ℗ and © 1993 Reunion Records. This song was inspired by 1 Kings 19:3–13 and Matthew 11:25–30.

Vince Antonucci is the founder and lead pastor of Forefront Church, an innovative church for the unchurched in Virginia Beach. Vince's passion is helping people find their way to God and creatively communicating biblical truth. He speaks at churches and conferences around the country and coaches church planters and church planting networks. He holds a degree in political science and philosophy from the University of Buffalo, and a master's degree from Cincinnati Bible Seminary. Vince is married to his best friend, Jennifer. They have two crazy awesome kids.